To: Shane + Elfe

Marriage...Why We Fight

fr: Bro Smith
1/Aug/2008

Copyright © 2007 Ainsley Reynolds
All rights reserved.
ISBN: 1-4196-6752-1
ISBN-13: 978-1419667527

Visit www.booksurge.com to order additional copies.

AINSLEY REYNOLDS

MARRIAGE... WHY WE FIGHT

2007

even # Marriage...Why We Fight

CONTENTS

Introduction xv
1. In the Beginning. 1
2. Why did God Make Adam without a Wife . . . 5
3. The Making of Eve 11
4. Ok then! What's Love got to do with it? 15
5. Jesus' Story!! Say what? 19
6. What does this mean?. 25
7. Marriage. 33
8. Our Story: Parts 1 & 2 37
9. What exactly do you want from me? 45
10. What's my Role?. 51
11. What's my Motivation? 57
12. You Know I Love you, Don't you? 69
13. Some Scary Stuff. 73
14. Satan's Mission 83
15. How will he do it? 87
16. What Shall your Response be?. 93
17. The Bride of Christ 101
18. How Should the Church Respond to
    Satan's Attack on Marriage 107
19. Becoming an Antidevil 111
20. The Grand Finale .117

ACKNOWLEDGEMENTS

There are no words adequate to express my appreciation and thanks to God for enabling me to complete this book. With all my heart I do say thanks to God for His help and for His faithfulness. To Him belong all the honor, glory and praise for what has been accomplished. While it is impossible to fully express to God the measure of gratitude and thanks He deserves, because His help is constant and new every morning, I would like to express my thanks to some of the people that He used to bring this about.

First and foremost, I must thank my wife Catherine Rose, my matchless flower, my gift from God and forever love. I thank you honey for your love, encouragement and support. Thanks for being my number one fan and critic. I thank you for being my helper on this project. I must especially thank not just you honey but also my daughter Kassandra and my son Eric for their sacrifices. Thank you for being understanding and giving me the time and space I needed to accomplish this. Thank you for your love. I love you.

Next, I would like to thank one of my editors, my sister-in-law, Professor Paulette Wilson PhD, founder and president of Berachah Ministries, conference speaker and author of such books as "In the Valley with a Promise", "Fruits of the Almond Tree" and many more. Thank you for refusing to allow me to settle for anything but my very best. Thank you for insisting that I take the time needed to deliver excellence. Thank you for verifying my references and demanding more. I pray that I have succeeded. I love and appreciate you my sister.

Special thanks to my other editor and dear friend, Mr. Keith Thompson, lecturer, president of PER Sports and author of "Heroes of the Hardcourt". Thank you for keeping my feet to the fire as you had promised. Thanks for all your editing help, and priceless advice. Thanks also to "Mr. Enforcer", Minister Quwan Ellis, teacher, and author of "Bruised but I Refuse to stay Broken", who promised to 'bruise and break' me if I did not get this book completed. Thank you for the support and encouragement and for also keeping my feet to the fire. I really appreciate and love you both.

I like the cover of this book. However, it is a vision I could never have realized without the help and expertise of some really wonderful people. First, I must thank Mrs. Tracy Thompson for her encouragement and for recommending to me the perfect couple Mr. and Mrs. Jamie and Jessica Mankowiski, and then bringing us together. Jamie and Jessica, beautiful in person and spirit, thank you for being my models. You were perfect. Next, I must thank my lighting specialist, my friend Mr. Thomas Shaw of Ruel's Video & Lighting who said to me "brother whatever you need just let me know".

Now the hardest part of this shoot was finding the weaponry to arm my couple. For this I must thank one of the truly nicest people I know, Mr. Rick Nelson, ex-marine, ex-police officer and great friend. The final look of the cover is not what was taken. All the background imagery is the work of graphic engineer and genius Mrs. Marcia Richardson. Thank you all for your talent, time, input and support. I greatly appreciate you.

I need to thank the First United Church family and my dear friend Bishop Lloyd Faulknor. Thank you for believing in me enough to appoint me to ministry which has helped to shape my destiny. I thank you all for always being there for Cathy and me and making sure we knew it. Thank you for your love, prayers and support.

Also, I must thank the House of Refuge church family for their love and support. You were my first pastoral assignment, a ministry dear to my heart. To my fellow laborers, Senior Pastor Joan Whittaker, and my fellow associate, Pastor Valretta Wilson, "the dynamic duo", to Bishop John Francis of Ruach Ministries who ordained us, thank you all for the privilege of serving, and for believing and investing in Cathy and me.

To all my friends, all those who've heard me speak at different conferences and encouraged me to write; and to all the couples that I have had the privilege of counseling over the years, who also encouraged me to write, I thank you for your encouragement and support. God bless you all.

All scriptures are taken from the Original King James version except where otherwise stated.

This Book Is Dedicated To The Glory Of God, In Loving Memory Of A Praying Mother, Viris Eunice Reynolds, Who Went Home To Be With Her Lord On April 11th 2007. I Am What I Am Today Because Of Her Unshakeable Faith In God And The Innumerable Prayers She Prayed For Her Children, Every One Of Which God Has Answered.

INTRODUCTION

Why even bother with marriage? This is the question some are now asking. We now have covenant marriages, regular / traditional marriages, open marriages, and gay marriages. We have a nation and its courts divided and in turmoil over what to do about the institution in general. There are many struggling to determine what is right and what is wrong, or what is acceptable and what is not. They are wrestling with the issue of civil unions, and whether it is fair or unfair.

While this debate continues, emotions run hot on both sides of the fence. Others are sitting in the middle saying enough already, just give everyone what they want and let us get on with life. (Can't we all just get along?) Then on the inside you have couples who awaken every day asking questions such as these:

If we both want it to work, why is it so hard? I thought I was supposed to enjoy this not endure it. And by the way, just how long am I supposed to put up with this?

Some have just concluded that life is too short to waste fighting for something that is not even worth fighting for. What's the big deal with marriage anyway?

To protect or not to protect, to redefine or not to redefine are some of the questions baffling our confused generation. The battle rages on in our classrooms, court rooms and bed rooms. Meanwhile, traditional marriage with its sky rocketing number of divorces seems to be heading the way of the dinosaurs. Some are thinking it is a failed experiment that has outlived its usefulness. Others see it as outdated, and in need of updating, an anachronism that is not worth fighting for.

Not long ago we saw Canada following in the footsteps of some European nations. They redefined the institution of marriage so that it no longer represents a union between one man and one woman. It can now be anything one desires; namely two men, two women or a man and woman. We see now in the United States of America organizations, groups, and forces of all kinds fighting desperately to follow suit to sign not just the death certificate of marriage, but to bury this God ordained institution. The institution presented throughout modern history as the only legitimate and lawful place for monogamous, heterosexual sexual intimacy.

One could argue the idea and say, no wonder society wants to get rid of marriage; it is preventing them from living how they want, doing what they want with whom they want. Nice try. We only have to turn on the television however to see that this is not so. Society not only already overindulges itself in every imaginable fantasy but it also has laws established to protect them.

Recently I read on the internet that one individual was seeking permission from another country to marry a dead person. I also read where one person actually got married to his car. We already have the Polyamorists in Canada and other countries demanding their right to marry. (Polyamorist are people who believe and practice the lifestyle of having many or more than one love/sex partners, with full knowledge and consent of all involved. *Dictionaty.com*) My guess is that all these are just the tip of the iceberg if some should have their way.

These crazy happenings have forced me to ask some point blank questions regarding marriage. *What is it really that we are fighting for? Where did it originate, and what exactly was the intent of its designer. What is its purpose? Why is it continually under attack, and why is it so hard to preserve?*

I believe it is wise to at least know what you have before you decide to throw it out. I therefore set out to find out what marriage is really about. Based on my findings I am now convinced that one of the main reasons why we are losing the battle for marriage is that we have no idea what it is we are fighting for, and why exactly it is worth fighting for. Many have become spectators and reluctant fighters in what we believe to be an irrelevant war. Consider the following.

A mighty hunter returning from the kill one day saw the people of his village weapons in hand, charging towards the hill and screaming. Dropping his kill he ran quickly to join them. Catching up to the group he asked a young man what's happening. To which the young man replied,

"Thieves, they have robbed the village and we are going to teach them a lesson".

The hunter staying towards the back continued with the group. He would help them if he needed to, but he kept going mainly out of curiosity. He wanted to see the outcome. After a while he decided this was not really his fight. He had not seen his family in days and should really go and see them. He missed them. These warriors could handle this. Before he broke off he asked another warrior, "What did they steal?" Recognizing him the warrior replied,

"While you were away bandits broke into your hut. They stole your possessions and kidnapped your family…"

Before he was finished speaking the mighty hunter was already charging through the large band of warriors. He was swift, silent and focused. In seconds he would be ahead of the pack and this time not because of curiosity. He now had a craving for vengeance with a thirst for blood. He now had a reason to fight; his purpose was harnessing all his skill, cunning, might and rage, focusing them on the hunt of his life. These thieves would not survive the night.

Like this hunter I am hoping to provide you with your reason to fight, by attempting to answer all the above questions and much more, like who is ultimately behind the attacks and why.

In this fresh, eye-opening look at marriage, we will examine where it came from and who established it. We will look at its purpose, and also get a Holy Spirit revealed, eye-opening look at what it represents, and was meant to symbolize on the earth.

In the end we will hopefully discover why all the uproar and whether or not it's worth the fight. The battle lines have been drawn; the war is on. Get ready to choose which side you are on. I believe, if we were to all recognize what is really at stake the enemy would not stand a chance.

CHAPTER 1

In The Beginning

1. **Where it all began.**

<u>Gen. 2: 15-25 (KJV)</u>

15. And the Lord God took the man, and put him into the garden of Eden to dress it and to keep it.

16. And the Lord God commanded the man, saying, Of every tree of the garden thou mayest freely eat:

17. But of the tree of the knowledge of good and evil, thou shalt not eat of it: for in the day that thou eatest thereof thou shalt surely die.

18. And the Lord God said, It is not good that the man should be alone; I will make him an help meet for him.

19. And out of the ground the Lord God formed every beast of the field, and every fowl of the air; and brought them unto Adam to see what he would call them: and whatsoever Adam called every living creature, that was the name thereof.

20. And Adam gave names to all cattle, and to the fowl of the air, and to every beast of the field; but for Adam there was not found an help meet for him.

21. And the Lord God caused a deep sleep to fall upon Adam, and he slept: and he took one of his ribs, and closed up the flesh instead thereof;

22. And the rib, which the Lord God had taken from man, made he a woman, and brought her unto the man.

23. And Adam said, This is now bone of my bones, and flesh of my flesh: she shall be called Woman, because she was taken out of Man.

24. Therefore shall a man leave his father and his mother, and shall cleave unto his wife: and they shall be one flesh.

25. And they were both naked, the man and his wife, and were not ashamed.

In these verses of scripture we see the first marriage ceremony performed when God presented the woman to Adam. This practice we see repeated over the centuries as fathers would present or give away their daughters in the Christian marriage ceremony. In the Christian wedding the minister will ask: "Who gives this woman to be wed?" The father will respond: "I do." This portion of the ceremony may seem odd or politically incorrect because how is it that there is no one giving away the son? Traditionally, the giving was always done by the father or a male member of the bride's family. It has become increasingly common however in many modern Christian marriages that the mother or both parents give the daughter away.

This seemingly insignificant role in the marriage ceremony also provides us with a link to its past and origin. The first link is to a not too distant past where girls were considered the property of their father. They therefore could be given away or sold. However, this practice did not start there, because even in cultures where the wife has to pay a dowry to the husband there is this concept of the father giving away his daughter. Usually the father is the one responsible for providing the dowry.

It can also be linked to a time when young ladies were being stolen from their families and forced to marry their abductors. The Christian ministers some say would ask this question to ensure that this was not the case.

Whichever age or culture you chose to tie the practice of fathers giving away their daughters to, a careful study will show that the practice predates it. The thinking and the reasoning behind this practice in different cultures have changed over the years. Each civilization's reason for doing its variation of the giving of the bride by her father may differ, but one thing is the same. They are all following a form of what they saw someone else did before them. The practice of the bride being given predates Christianity. It traces all the way back to God in the Garden of Eden.

This practice symbolizes or commemorates God's role in the first marriage. It is like a reminder that it was all started or instituted by God. In other words, marriage was God's idea. This small portion of ceremony is a reenactment of God's first wedding. The proof that a wedding or marriage occurred in the Garden of Eden is also evident by the fact that in Gen. 3 verse 6 Adam is afterwards referred to as husband, and in verse 8 they are referred to as Adam and his wife.

More compelling proof can be found in the New Testament coming straight from the lips of Jesus. Jesus was responding to a question regarding divorce posed to him by the Pharisees. In His response in Mark 10:6-8 Jesus said,

But from the beginning of the creation *God made them male and female.*

⁷For this cause shall a man leave his father and mother, and cleave to his wife;

⁸And they twain shall be one flesh: so then they are no more twain, but one flesh.

With the phrase "from the beginning of creation" Jesus clearly establishes that in the Garden of Eden, the very beginning, God made a male and female, a man and a woman for the purpose of marriage.

While all other creatures were made in abundance, God created one man and one woman in His likeness, He then joined them in marriage and all of humanity was produced by this union. Thus God invented or established marriage before anything else to do with man was done. God had His reasons for this and like everything else He did they were good reasons. We will examine these later.

These are realities that have not slipped by the enemy of marriage however, as he works towards the total destruction of marriage. He will deceive and trick us into gutting it of its godly symbolisms and references until his final victory and marriage hopefully becomes a thing of the past. The fact that God instituted marriage is not the reason for the enemy's all consuming hatred for the institution. We will uncover his true reason when we see the true symbolic representation of marriage on the earth. This we are going to do by answering a number of "why" questions beginning with…

CHAPTER 2

Why did God Make Adam without a Wife?

Many are the possible answers one might expect to such a question. Many however can be ruled out by carefully examining the character and nature of God. We know from scripture that He intended to make woman; therefore, she was not an after thought. Heb. 4:3 speaks of the works being finished from before the foundation of the world therefore she was a part of it from before the beginning. We know that God did not have an 'oops' moment and when He was finished He looked and said:

"Goodness, gracious Almighty Me! I forgot to make the woman. Sorry Adam. I'll fix."

We are left with an all-wise God creating a fully functioning male adult. He then places him in a garden paradise with no female counterpart. He went further, surrounding him with every creature having both male and female counterparts, just in case he may fail to realize what he was missing. Knowing that spring brings out the romance in us, what was God thinking? Talk about loneliness and torture, poor Adam.

Throughout the scriptures we see many examples of God's amazing attention to detail. Consider for example King Herod ordering a census at the time of Jesus' birth, causing Joseph to move his nine-month pregnant wife many miles to fulfill a prophecy. Jesus was to be born in Bethlehem. We see also the Pharaoh's daughter finding Moses in the river. She just happened to be one of the only women in Egypt with the power to preserve the life of a Hebrew male child. She also just happened to have the means to educate and equip him with the skills needed to later manage the greatest relocation of people ever. God does not miss a thing. So then, what's going on with Adam's predicament? I believe the answer to this question is three fold, and all a part of God's carefully designed plan.

1—Responsibility

The first reason for Adam not being created with a wife at the start has to do with responsibility. A man must first be introduced to work and responsibility before he is introduced to a wife. He had to tend the garden (labor) *Gen. 2:15* and name the animals (administration) *Gen. 2:19-20*. It was in the process of carrying out these duties that he discovered that there was none other like him. Can you imagine the disappointment?

A man who is not first introduced to work and responsibility before a wife will enter marriage looking for a mother or worse a maid. A man entering marriage embraces the greatest responsibility of his life: another life. A man who has not worked a day in his life, or proven himself capable of taking care of even a pet hamster, should not be entrusted with the life of another person, another man's daughter that he has poured his life into raising.

Marriage is work, and a husband is expected to provide for, protect, nurture and lead his family. A child is trained on plastic cups before he is given glass and crystal. We as parents demand that our children prove themselves capable and responsible and have a valid driver's license before we will hand them the car keys and say: 'Have a good time'. How then can we allow an untested or unproven, irresponsible man or boy to walk off with our daughters and say: 'Have a good life'.

God is a responsible Father indeed and He missed no detail in modeling for us the way it should be done, when He performed the first marriage. Adam was therefore created, put to work and his performance monitored before he was given a wife. Jesus puts it this way: "*He who is faithful in little things shall be entrusted with much.*" Matt. 25:21.

2—Headship

I believe God's second reason for creating Adam without a wife in the beginning, has to do with the role God intended for the man, the role of head or leader of the family. This role has nothing to do with inferiority or superiority but rather like positions in a company or organization, they are assigned as the owner sees fit. We see God's wisdom displayed, in that by placing Adam in the garden first to name the animals and tend the garden, he allows Adam to develop a knowledge and understanding of his environment and surroundings, before Eve is brought into the picture.

When Eve is made and then presented to Adam, by default, his would be the responsibility to teach her the names he had given each of the animals. He would also have to point out details and protect her from any dangers he may have discovered. Eve in turn would learn to trust his wisdom and rely on him. Look at it if you please in light of how the West was won. Whoever got there first and staked their claim was the owner. (Though in Adam and Eve's case he was more like head caretaker because God owned everything). It can also be compared with seniority on a job. Then add to this the fact that there is no sin, meaning no greed, no lust, no selfishness and no envy. This means it was a good thing for Eve too.

No organization, regardless how large or how small, can survive without clearly defined roles. Neither can the family. God knew this, and so by design He created and established the roles of each in the family. God's design intended for man to be the leader or head of his family: the protector and provider. God made man physically stronger. By his very design a man should know that the more strenuous and demanding roles in the family are his. I therefore believe it is crucial that a man cover certain basics and accomplish certain things before he even begins to look for a wife.

Too many women today carry much more than their fair share because too many men fail to adequately prepare for a family before they begin one. A young man with no job, no career or means of providing for himself and no place of his own, does not need to get a wife. He needs to get a *life*. A man in this position looking for a wife does not seek to fulfill his God given role as head, protector and provider for a family. He is either simply looking for legal sex or for a woman to take care of him. We are as a result left with so many fatherless homes, because once the reality, the pressures and the responsibility of headship hits them, many abandon their families. They are off and running, in an effort to continue their life of irresponsibility and selfishness.

3—Value

Reason number three is, I believe, the most important, because it speaks of the value that God places on the woman and also intended for Adam to place on her. The value of most things are usually determined by various factors. The primary factor is the ratio of supply and demand. Another is the process by which the thing is made or developed, by this I speak of quality instead of quantity. Whether a thing is plentiful or not, people will pay more for a particular brand if they believe it is better.

Let us look for example at a girl's best friend, a diamond. What is it that makes a diamond so expensive? I have seen finely cut glass and cubic zirconium deceive many, because they were polished, cut and set in jewelry to look like diamonds. If they have the same appearance, (and jewelry is for appearances), why is it that diamonds are so expensive when compared to these other stones or glass?

Going back to our determining factors we find the answers. The first reason is, diamonds are very scarce and found only in certain parts of the world. Secondly, the process to locate and extract the ore, then cut and polish it, until it sparkles the way every girl likes it is a very arduous and complex one. Those who desire to posses a diamond must therefore be willing to pay the price in labor or cash.

Another very important thing about our valuables is the fact that we treat them differently. The words that come to mind when thinking of the way we treat our valuables is "cherish" or "treasure". We insure them, rent or buy special boxes or houses to keep them and spend even more money to have them serviced.

Geneses 1:20 tells us that the other creatures were created in abundance after their kind, but God only made one man and one woman. In addition, the process that created Eve involved surgery for Adam and was unique in comparison to all of God's other creations. God who does not miss any detail is obviously up to something, and whatever it is, it also has to do with Adam's valuing of Eve.

Consider also this: How much would you pay for a glass of water in a restaurant? Most of us expect it to be free, so a nominal fee at most. Now in contrast, how much would you pay for a glass of water after crossing the desert for two weeks without having even one drop to drink? I submit that you would probably give all you have including your clothes and shoes. It is also a known fact that longing, need and desperate desire significantly increases the value of the desired object.

The more available a product is the cheaper the product. This truth supports a statement I have heard the older folks say. They would often say that a woman that is too readily available (for a man's pleasure) is cheap and will be treated as such.

God in His wisdom designed it so that Adam would develop a desperate need and painful longing. This brought on by his loneliness, accentuated by his garden paradise, in which every other creature or animal is paired with its respective female counter part. Though it is not clear whether or not Adam knew what exactly he needed, God knew his heart, his true need and longing. God then filled it by creating Eve. Adam then responded as intended by loving her above all else and valuing her above all others.

CHAPTER 3

The Making of Eve

The question here becomes: Why was Eve's making different from all other creature, in that she was made from a rib removed from the side of Adam? *Gen.2: 19-22*. Unlike all other creatures formed directly from the dust Eve was formed from something removed from the anatomy of Adam.

The part taken from Adam's anatomy and the process used for its removal is significant in terms of what it mirrors and represents. However, this significance is not to Adam but to God. I doubt very much that Adam had counted his ribs. Adam therefore did not awake from his sleep feeling reduced or deficient, mindful of something missing or lacking and desiring it back. Neither did it cause him to love Eve more because a rib as opposed to a head, neck, shoulder or foot bone was used. The intent here was to have Adam 'give birth' to his wife, and of course without sin there was no pain involved.

You may have heard the expression "a face only a mother could love." This expression comes from the fact that when a normal woman gives birth that baby comes out looking kind of weird, wrinkled, crumpled and messy. To that mother, however, a more beautiful baby has never been born. She is in love. She is hooked, sucked in and unable to help herself. A mother will run into a burning building or before a moving vehicle without thought, to save her baby. That is love.

God by design ensured that Adam would be helplessly and hopelessly in love with Eve, by causing him to give birth to her. Hence his expression: "This is now bone of my bones, and flesh of my flesh." Many men refer to their wife as their baby. Though the origin of this practice is unsure, Eve was indeed, Adam's baby. Like a mother who was told for years that she cannot have children, finally giving birth to her first child, she does not care what it looks like as long as it breathes. She is in love.

It has been said that Eve was the perfect figure of a woman and she was. The question then becomes perfect for whom? Or what does that look like. The reality is, our tastes differ. Some men like their women fat, some tall, some short and some like them skinny. The women of the Mursi and Surma tribes in southern Ethiopia split and stretch their lower lips with discs. Their men believe that the larger the lip the more beautiful the woman. We probably consider perfection from Hollywood's point of view, but considering that Adam had none before to compare her with, what was his preference?

The fact is people with healthy self-esteem usually use themselves as their standard of beauty. Again we see the infinite wisdom of God as He covers every variable or contingency. By having Adam give birth to Eve, his DNA formed her; she would therefore be his perfect counterpart, looking like whatever he looked like. (It can be said that this was not necessary, because Adam would be attracted to her regardless of looks, simply because she was the only other human. Maybe, what God had in mind would require more than attraction and His attention to detail missed nothing). Adam was indeed hopelessly and helplessly in love, with a built in desire to nurture and protect Eve his baby.

Now all this attention to detail by God is for a reason. It was crucial that Adam not just use Eve to satisfy his needs or treat her like just another of the animals, but rather that he love her unconditionally. This is the kind of love represented in the marriage vow by the phrase "for richer, for poorer, in sickness and in health, until death do us part" I know of no place in scripture where wives are commanded to love their husband. I see however in Eph. 5:25 and Col. 3:19 where husbands are commanded to love their wives.

Someone may interject at this point to ask why all the drama. If God wanted them to do something specific why couldn't He just make them both, place them in the garden and say to them,

"Listen up you two. This is what I would like you to do. Get it? Good. Have a good time."

He couldn't because you can't legislate or command love. You can command respect or demand reverence but not love. The romantic or romance expert will tell you, you can create the environment, the situation or the circumstances for someone to fall in love with you or someone else, but you cannot command love.

We know this because God Himself demonstrated this for us. God tried to command the love of Israel when He issued the 10 commandments. The first one was God's attempt to command love. Deut. 6:1-6.

⁵And thou shalt love the LORD thy God with all thine heart, and with all thy soul, and with all thy might.

This approach did not work. He spoke about it in Isaiah 29:13.

*Wherefore the Lord said, Forasmuch as this people draw near me with their mouth, and with their lips do honor me, **but have removed their heart far from me**, and their fear toward me is taught by the precept of men:*

In other words God said they have been taught to fear me, trained to reverence and honor me, by saying and doing all the right things, but there is no love, because their hearts are not in it. Rather it is removed far from me. They have done what I've commanded, but it has not delivered what I desired. What they did is called going through the motions or lip service.

After the failure of that approach God tried another when He appeared in the person of Jesus Christ. The bible says in St. John 3:16 *"For God so loved the world that He gave His only begotten Son...."* This time around He first demonstrates His love and then says in St. John 14:15 *"If ye love me, keep my commandments".* Note God's new approach. Now He asks us to love Him first and if we do then we are to prove it with our obedience.

God now looks for the sincere heart first. If the love is genuine, He then says the command I now give you based on your declaration of love for Me is that you love one another as I have loved you. This is a much different approach, and now we see people voluntarily and willingly laying down their lives for Him. Oh what love!

Having established that there is purpose behind everything that God does, one thing is clear thus far: Whatever God's plan, whatever His purpose or intent, whatever He was developing in the Garden of Eden it hinged on, depended on, and had everything to do with *love*.

CHAPTER 4

Ok then! What's love got to do with it?

Knowing that everything God does has a divine purpose, all this talk about love and the need for Adam to love his wife, leads us to the obvious next question. Why? Why is love so important to God's plan? The answer to this question lies in what love accomplished in the garden.

The bible tells us in 1Tim. 2:14. *"And Adam was not deceived, but the woman being deceived was in the transgression"*. Eve was deceived but Adam was not. Satan was able to convince Eve that God lied. Gen. 3: 4.

And the serpent said unto the woman, Ye shall not surely die: 5. For God doth know that in the day ye eat thereof, then your eyes shall be opened, and ye shall be as gods, knowing good and evil.

Satan was able to convince Eve that she would not die, that God's real reason for not wanting them to eat of the tree was to keep them inferior to Himself and foolish. However, the bible said Adam was not deceived and this I believe to be crucial, for herein lies the genius of God and the power of love.

'Adam was not deceived', meaning that with the perfect intellect God had given him, coupled with his knowledge and understanding of God, he knew without a doubt that God would deliver on His promise. He knew he would die once he ate the fruit. Deceive means to 'trick, mislead or falsely persuade, which is to cause someone to believe what is not true' (**Dictionary.com & American Heritage Dic.**). If this was not the case with Adam, then he ate the fruit knowing that he was going to die.

Adam was therefore very much aware that it did not matter what knowledge or revelation the fruit produced if it would also kill him. A man with his understanding would also have realized that it did not matter if the fruit opened his eyes, if they would shortly thereafter be closed forever. Yet he still ate the fruit. If we are to believe anything other than the above then we are saying that Adam also was deceived; and if he was, then the bible is wrong. I don't think so. What then are we looking at?

We are seeing Adam laying down his life for his wife. To say maybe he believed he would live, is to say he too was deceived and the bible clearly says he was not. *1Tim. 2:14.* What we have is Adam choosing to die rather than to remain in paradise without Eve. Adam had come to love Eve so much that rather than return to being alone or receive a replacement he willingly laid down his life. We see Adam's love for Eve was such that he willingly embraced whatever would befall her rather than continue without her. Though it meant being separated from the fellowship he enjoyed with God, he still chose to die, for so great was his love for his wife.

One may venture to argue that maybe Adam did not know what Eve was giving him to eat. Nice try, but not so. First, this is the Adam who tended the garden before Eve came along. He named every creature, and knew every tree and fruit, being vegetarian at that time. Also we see in John 15:22.

If I had not come and spoken unto them, they had not had sin: but now they have no cloke for their sin.

Here Jesus stated that had He not spoken to the Jews then they would not have sinned. Sin is always a choice. Otherwise we could argue that God's judgment is not just. Adam had to make a choice, and his love for Eve was his undoing as it is for all of us. What we love usually is the means to our undoing.

Be very careful who or what you fall for because it will have the power to become your undoing. This was the case with Samson who fell for Delilah. *Judges 16:4*. This love ultimately cost him his eye sight, his strength, and his freedom. The bible therefore warns us to 'set our affection on things above…' Col. 3:2. Love chose for Adam and the choice was to lay down his life for his wife. John 15:13.

Greater love hath no man than this that a man lay down his life for his friends.

What has love got to do with it? Everything. It's all about love, and still there is more. There is a whole lot more to this story than I was told. The fact is it is Jesus' story from cover to cover. The bible is His-story. It's all about Jesus Christ.

CHAPTER 5

Jesus' story!! Say what?

As a child in Sunday school I was taught that the story of Adam and Eve is the story of original sin and how God made man. When I got to high school however the jury came back on the making of man portion and enlightened me by way of my priest. He explained that the story of Adam and Eve was not real but rather made up to explain original sin. He further explained that we evolved from monkeys and that there is proof. (Tempting, but I won't touch that here). He concluded by saying, this does not reduce or make God any less God because this happens to be the way He chose to create.

Back then, I was totally confused and thought: well, I guess it could be. Now however, I know better, and that his teachings were nothing but a lot of "monkey's dribble". If the priest's story were true it would absolutely reduce or eliminate God. The first thing it would do is it would make God a liar because He introduced Himself by claiming to do what He didn't. God continued later in the bible by saying He is not a man and does not lie. *Num. 23:19.* You are about to understand, however, why it would be important to Satan to negate the story of Adam and Eve, or as he did with Eve, try to convince us that God is a liar.

In the book of 1 Corinthians 15:45-47, Jesus is referred to as the last Adam. Now the reason why this story of Adam and

Eve like many other stories is recorded in the bible is this; it is there because it foretells in some way the life of Jesus Christ. This story of Adam and Eve does so more than any other to the extent that Jesus is called the last Adam. Satan therefore hates it with a passion and here is why.

The first thing we note is, just as Adam sacrificed the paradise of Eden to go after his wife, Jesus loved us so much that rather than remaining in the indescribable splendor and glory of heaven without us, He embraced sin's consequences, the ultimate being death and came after us.

Next, we see Adam put to sleep and his wife formed from a rib removed from his side. Jesus too was put to sleep on a cross. This is consistent with scripture in that Jesus throughout His ministry referred to death as sleep. *Matt. 9:24 and John 11:11.* This was first done by God speaking to Moses of his death in Deut. 31:16. Death is therefore a form of sleep. Just as Adam was put to sleep by God so too was Jesus. This is confirmed in St. John 10:17-18.

*Therefore doth my Father love me, because I lay down my life, that I might take it again. 18**. No man taketh it from me, but I lay it down of myself**. I have power to lay it down, and I have power to take it again. This commandment have I received of my Father.*

His bride the church was then formed from that which was taken from His side.

Herein lies the significance of the rib being used to form Eve. For a rib to be taken, an opening or hole must be made in Adam's side for its removal. This is clearly indicated in Gen. 2:21 by the phrase "and closed up the flesh instead of". Just as Eve was formed from that rib pulled from Adam's side, so too the church received life and came to be from the blood that came out of Jesus' side. This occurred after He was put to sleep on the cross. His side was then opened with a soldier's spear, and out came the blood that gave life to His bride. *John 19:33-34.*

Entire books have been written on this subject of the life giving blood of Jesus Christ, and every Christian knows that outside of the blood of Jesus Christ there is no life, no salvation, no church and therefore no bride of Christ. They also know that the church or the bride of Christ is not joined, but rather you must be born in it, hence the expression, the new birth, or born again as in St. John 3:3. This is accomplished through baptism in Jesus Christ. *Gal. 3:27, 1 Cor. 12:13* This also is why the blood is given so much significance in Jewish laws, sacrifices, and customs recorded in the Old Testament because all reference Jesus Christ.

Now if we must be born again, which is the expression used by Jesus in St. John 3:3 to describe our change, and the person giving us life is Jesus, we can therefore say that Jesus gave birth to his bride. This confirms what I described earlier in the making of Eve that the operation God performed when he removed Adam's rib to form Eve represented Adam giving birth to his bride.

Here again we see Adam made to mirror Christ with one significant difference. Eve's birth was painless to Adam because as yet there was no sin in the world. Our birth was to Jesus the extreme opposite. After the fall, God pronounced a sentence on the woman in Gen 3:1 that in pain she would bring forth children. The understanding here is that God made women throughout time to sample a small portion of the extreme pain that Jesus would experience, in redeeming us from the death disobedience had sentenced us to. This also is why throughout the bible extreme pain and suffering is compared to a woman in travail or a woman giving birth. This in turn points to the unspeakable pain that Christ would experience for us, since the pain of childbirth is a mere shadow of His torture and crucifixion, the price of our freedom.

Highlighted and underlined above in St. John 10:18 is the clause *"no man takes it from me, but I lay it down of myself"*. This statement by Jesus clearly shows that His death was His choice. He was not made to do it or tricked into it, but rather chose to do it despite all the horror and pain of the crucifixion that would include separation from His Father. He still chose to endure it because of His love for us.

The metaphor used to describe the choice Jesus had to make is that of a cup containing pain, suffering and death. His choice was to drink or not to drink. Matt. 20:22 & 26:39, or St. John. 18: 11.

Then said Jesus unto Peter, Put up thy sword into the sheath: the cup which my Father hath given me, shall I not drink it?

Adams mirroring of this was his choice to eat or not to eat the fruit, despite the consequences of which he was fully aware. God's attention to detail ensured that Adam's action too was a matter of choice. And like Jesus he willingly chose to eat the fruit because of his love for Eve.

One other nugget in regards to God's detail is the fact that Adam's moment of decision occurred in a garden called Eden, and Jesus' occurred in one called Gethsemane. (One major difference between the two is that, while Jesus' choice was not a sin, Adam's choice definitely was, as it always is when we disobey God's command).

Even as Jesus' decision was a matter of choice, for Adam to be a true representation of Jesus he could not have been tricked or deceived by Satan but rather it also had to have been a choice. Also he had to be motivated purely by love. He could not have done it for the knowledge, or to be like God. He was already like God, created in His image and likeness. Those are all selfish reasons. It had to be for love. This would explain why God went through all the details He did. They were to ensure that Adam was totally, helplessly and unconditionally in love with Eve. Jesus' story is all about love: God's amazing inexplicable love for us.

Though there are other parallels between Adam and Jesus that could be pointed out, the last one I will use for the sake of our discussion is that of Eve being presented to Adam by God. My reason for mentioning this last is because for Christ this has not yet occurred. It is however clearly described in 1 Thessalonians 4:16-17.

> *16. For the Lord himself shall descend from heaven with a shout, with the voice of the archangel, and with the trump of God: and the dead in Christ shall rise first: 17. Then we which are alive and remain shall be caught up together with them in the clouds, to meet the Lord in the air: and so shall we ever be with the Lord.*

In the same way that the Spirit of God presented to Adam his bride, so too God will present everyone that is filled with the Holy Spirit to Jesus in the air. This event is what the Church refers to, with the term "rapture". Further proof or confirmation that this is what is being symbolized is the fact that this event will be followed by what is called the Marriage Supper of the Lamb in Rev. 19:8-9. Another name for the rapture could be the presentation of the bride.

The bible speaks of Adam and Eve then being naked and not ashamed. This reflects or speaks of the opening of the eyes of the believers. 1 Cor. 13:12 describes our awakening and the transparency that will exist afterwards, when we will know even as we are known. It can also be likened to the removal of a bride's veil after the vows, so they are now able to see each other clearly. This is reiterated by the fact that Adam and Eve's intimacy is referred to as Adam knowing Eve. *Gen. 4:1*

Contrary to that which I was taught as a child and what Satan would have us believe, the story of Adam and Eve, apart from being very real is about much more than original sin. Regarding that monkey business, I will not waste time to add credence to stupidity by commenting on it in this text. The story of Adam and Eve like the story of Joseph, Joshua, Moses, David, Isaac and many others, are included in the bible because in some way by design, God caused their lives, or recorded experiences to point to, speak of, or mirror the life or person of Jesus Christ.

CHAPTER 6

What does this mean?

The understanding of what this all means will require a brief overview of some of the early works of God. We need to look at other patterns and consistencies that may grant us a glimpse into what this entire first marriage story was all about.

One of God's consistencies as revealed in scripture is His use of symbols as memorials, reminders and references. From the establishing of the rainbow to the Lord's Supper, He consistently uses symbols and without exception, He takes them all seriously!

A quick overview of memorials will show us the following.

- The Sabbath day was established as a reminder that He rested on that day and that we will also one day rest from our labor. *Gen. 2:2 & Ex. 20:8.*
- The rainbow He established was a symbolic reminder to us and to Him that he would never again destroy this world by water. *Gen 9:13-16.*
- God had the Israelites established annual Passover Feasts and celebrations as a reminder of how their liberation from bondage and their exodus from Egypt were accomplished by Him. *Ex. 12:24-27*
- The memorial stones removed from the middle of Jordan and set up in Canaan, to remind them that

the waters of Jordan also were rolled back for them to cross. *Josh. 4:1-7.*
- The lights and stars in the heavens we see in *Gen .1:14* God saying *'let them be for signs and seasons'.*
- The Lord's Supper established by Jesus, He told us, that as often as we observe it we commemorate His death, (the cost of our freedom) until He returns. *Luke 22:19*
- The entire Jewish Priesthood and all it entailed, its sacrifices, offerings and structure are all symbolic representations of God's intent or plan for humanity through Jesus Christ.

It is evident that for whatever His reason, God used these symbolic representations, memorials, or reminders, and has passed this practice on to us. When we consider these factors, coupled with Malachi 3:6. *For I am the Lord, I change not,* I am forced to conclude that one of the most important symbols established on this earth by God is the one most overlooked. It is overlooked in terms of its importance, its representation and its meaning. This symbol is the marriage union between a man and a woman or husband and wife. Marriage is so significant a symbol or reminder to God that before He did anything with mankind this institution or reminder was put in place.

This significance that God places on marriage is further underscored throughout scriptures with statements like,

> Proverbs 18:22 *Whoso findeth a wife findeth a good thing,* ***and obtaineth favour of the Lord.***
> 1 Peter 3:7 *Likewise, ye husbands, dwell with them according to knowledge, giving honor unto the wife, as unto the weaker vessel, and as being heirs together of the grace of life;* ***that your prayers be not hindered.***

"Your prayers not hindered or blocked" implies that if we are "messing up" this sacred union God does not even care to hear from us. Now that is serious. (See also Mark 10:2-12 & Eccl. 9:9).

I would have to say that the most revealing scripture regarding this is,

> Ephesians 5:22-33. [31]*For this cause shall a man leave his father and mother, and shall be joined unto his wife, and they two shall be one flesh.* [32]***This is a great mystery: but I speak concerning Christ and the church.***

Here Paul outlines this parallel and the true meaning of this symbol of marriage.

Now do not miss this next point because I believe this is where we are going as a nation. Another constant that I have observed in scripture regarding marriage is this. Every nation that has destroyed, corrupted, or removed this symbol as God established it, was shortly after destroyed or removed by God. We see this from Sodom to Rome and will see it again. This is made clear also when He had the children of Israel destroy all the people and nations of Canaan and possessed their lands.

> Deut.9:4. *Speak not thou in thine heart, after that the Lord thy God hath cast them out from before thee, saying, For my righteousness the Lord hath brought me in to possess this land: but for the wickedness of these nations the Lord doth drive them out from before thee.*
> 5. *Not for thy righteousness, or for the uprightness of thine heart, dost thou go to possess their land: but for the wickedness of these nations the Lord thy God doth drive them out from before thee, and that he may perform the word which the Lord swore unto thy fathers, Abraham, Isaac, and Jacob.*

> Jeremiah 5:8-9. *They were as fed horses in the morning: <u>every one neighed after his neighbor's wife</u>. 9. **Shall I not visit for these things? saith the Lord: and shall not my soul be avenged on such a nation as this?***
> Ezekiel 33:26. *Ye stand upon your sword, ye work abomination, <u>and ye defile every one his neighbor's wife</u>: **and shall ye possess the land?***

(It seems to me that whenever mankind rejects God and His laws we end up going in two seemingly opposite directions at the same time. We will corrupt ourselves with all manner of below animalistic, humanity debasing sexual perversions, and indulge in unspeakably acts of evil, depravity and barbarism. At the same time we will make strange gods unto ourselves and of ourselves. Therefore, as we see ourselves as gods apart from God we become in actuality even worse than beasts).

I believe those fighting for the preservation of marriage fight for a whole lot more than just our families. We fight for our civilization, our culture, the very survival of a nation. All of humanity started with the marriage of one man and a woman. The family is to humanity what the atom is to the universe.

All matter in the universe is made up of atoms. These are particles so tiny that they cannot be observed even under a microscope. The atom resembles a miniature solar system. In the center of the atom is the nucleus around which electrons orbit like planets around the sun. The nucleus or core is composed of protons (positive charge) and neutrons (negative charge) particles. Around this center tiny electrons move around in their orbit.

This is now my picture of a family. Its core is comprised of the parents the father (male) the mother (female) and the children running around.

MARRIAGE...WHY WE FIGHT

The splitting of an atoms nucleus into two or more smaller nuclei is called fission. Most atoms will not fission because a binding force or energy that holds its protons and neutrons together prevents it. However, there are some atoms with big unstable nuclei, like uranium (U-235) that can be split apart, under certain conditions. This discovery ushered in the atomic age of man.

The energy or force that is released from the sustained, continuous, uncontrolled, splitting of nuclei is referred to as an atomic or nuclear explosion. The splitting of the nuclei as in the case of the nuclear bomb will destroy not only the element but everything within hundreds of miles. The destruction is not just immediate. The process will produce radiation that will keep on killing and destroying in different ways for tens if not hundreds of years.

This too is a picture of the family. The forceful splitting of the nucleus is called divorce. The man and the woman in a marriage were meant to be inseparable, held together by a force that prevents it. That force is called love. However, there are those that will separate when circumstances create instability, weakening the force that binds them.

The destructive force released by divorce among humanity is like the destructive force of the nuclear bomb on nature. Homes disintegrate, families dissolve, hearts are shattered, dreams die, children are emotionally disfigured and set on course to continue the splitting, ensuring that the fallout like nuclear radiation will continue destroying for years. Friends become foes; in-laws become outlaws in an ever widening circle of dead and walking wounded as love turns to hate. All this and more caused by the splitting of humanity's nucleus or divorce.

The fact is that the ingredients needed to maintain marriage as God designed it are the very same ingredients that serve to preserve a civilize society. I speak of ingredients such as love, fidelity, integrity, courage and commitment to name a few. Also the fact that almost 90% of those in our jails or prisons are from broken homes should sound an alarm.

The marriage is the foundation on which the family is built. The family in turn is the building block of the society. Statistics have shown that the poorest segment of our society has the lowest number of marriages. This segment also accounts for the greatest number of illiterates and has overall lower educational achievements. If nearly ninety percent of inmates are from broken homes, this can only mean that it gets worse. It means, the breakdown of marriage ultimately leads to increase in abortions, drugs, prostitution, thefts, murders, gangs and so on.

The conditions created when marriages crumble and families self-destruct are the festering seething bed for every evil and depravity that begs for God,s judgment. When you separate the inseparable something gets broken. Broken marriages create broken families, broken families produce broken people. If those who are whole are barely making it, what chance do the broken have?

What we are also accomplishing by destroying marriage is, we are recreating the very societies that God in scripture said He absolutely could not tolerate and had to destroy. For more proof simply examine some of the worse communities you know; check the census statistics for number of marriages, divorces, out of wedlock births and single parent homes. Next, compare it with the statistics for great communities and you'll have more proof. (This information is easily obtainable on the web. I would rather you do your own checking using communities you know, lest you believe I've selected token communities simply to validate my argument).

Beyond protecting us from total societal collapse, the sacred purpose of marriage as God's symbolic reminder can be seen in this. When someone ties a string around his or her finger as a reminder to do something such as taking out the trash, once the task is accomplished or if there is no trash the string is removed and tossed. The bible clearly teaches that there is no salvation in the grave, meaning a person cannot get saved after they have died. This is why the marriage vows are until death. The surviving spouse is free.

In Colossians 2:14 the bible tells us that the ordinances were nailed to the cross with Christ. They were all abolished or rather fulfilled in Jesus, like the string on the finger; once the task is accomplished the ordinances were tossed. This again shows that it is all about Jesus, every bit of it.

Animals are no longer offered up to God as sacrifices in temples, because what that was meant to symbolize has been accomplished. There are no couples after death because God no longer needs a reminder: the so called string on God's finger is gone when death occurs. Salvation is for the living. The time to get to know Jesus as savior and Lord is now. All the prayers in the world will not save someone after they are dead if they rejected Jesus while they were alive.

Note this response by Jesus in Mark 12:19

Master, Moses wrote unto us, If a man's brother die, and leave his wife behind him, and leave no children, that his brother should take his wife, and raise up seed unto his brother. 20. Now there were seven brethren: and the first took a wife, and dying left no seed. 21. And the second took her, and died, neither left he any seed: and the third likewise. 22. And the seven had her, and left no seed: last of all the woman died also. 23. In the resurrection therefore, when they shall rise, whose wife shall she be of them? For the seven had her to wife. 24. And Jesus answering said unto them, *Do ye not therefore err, because ye know not the scriptures, neither the power of God? 25. For when they shall rise from the dead, they neither marry, nor are given in marriage; but are as the angels which are in heaven.*

Marriage does not exist outside of mankind; not among angels, the dead or among any other creature. Mankind has sinned against God and is in need of redemption or face destruction for our sins. Marriage is the symbolic reminder placed among men by God to remind Him of His intent to redeem man. Therefore, removing or destroying it is like saying to God: "We don't need Your redemption."

We have removed the 'string' from His finger, and invited upon ourselves the wrath and awesome judgment of God, and (believe me when I tell you this) He delivers.

The battle to save marriage as God designed it is more important than the war against terrorism. When God is for you and is your defender, though the terrorists may try 1000 ways to harm you they will not even get close. When God however comes after you nothing in heaven, earth, or hell can save or help you.

Let us keep the string on His finger.

CHAPTER 7

Marriage

Families have been the cornerstone of every culture and civilization on the earth for over 6000 years. The institution of marriage has been the cement or foundation on which the corner stone is set. History has taught that if we "mess" with the cement or foundation the corner stone becomes unstable or dislodged and the entire building crumbles to the ground. This we have seen with so many civilizations before us who tampered with this sacred institution. We saw that even before God removed them their society suffered severe breakdown and decay. Still we continue to march in the same direction towards God's judgment with alarming statistics that indicate more people are choosing to cohabitate than marry. Then of those who do get married, more fail or end in divorce than those that succeed. We now also have many practicing that which God considers abominable, flaunting and promoting their lifestyle, with pride, and boldly declaring, "We want to be married too". (We'll examine this later).

Many who are already married wake up daily with a knot in their stomachs and pain in their chests. They are asking, "What am I doing wrong, where is the happily-ever-after?" Some couples conclude: *we must not be right for each other, because no way could it be this hard.* Others simply struggle day after day trying to figure out how long to hang on, and when exactly to say enough is enough. Some who are nobler have resolved that they will stay together for the kids, with an understanding that the marriage is a front and does not really exist.

Sadly however, for a large majority when the challenges, tests and attacks that inevitably hit every marriage come, they simply call it quits. They conclude: *life is too short; we made a mistake. This is not working; I'll just move on and keep looking until I find Mr. or Miss Right.* They say: *I refuse to be unhappy.* With frustration at an all time high, the divorce rate continues to rise despite the paralyzing anguish it produces in the lives of its victims, causing many afterwards to struggle just to keep on living.

Despite all the failures, when we see the successes they are so ideal and wonderful we can't help but dream and try for it. Still we ask ourselves, what is it that couples who seem to get it right and seem to have it all together know that everyone else does not? The first thing many of them would tell you is there is more to marriage than saying "I do".

I remember my first time watching my oldest brother play basketball. The game seemed like fun. I really liked it, and thought I would give it a try. Right after I had it all figured out I joined in. It was not long after I had gotten into the game that I was getting out, totally frustrated and calling it a stupid game. While I was watching they made it look so easy.

The fact that I could not get the ball through the hoop was just one of my problems. I tried my best, yet everything I did they kept telling me I was wrong. You can't dribble with two hands like that. Ok then, I'll just run to the hoop with it. You can't do that; that's traveling; that's goal tending; that's a foul; that's interference. This game was a lot harder than it appeared. When I got tired of them going around me with the ball as if I was not there I started kicking it. You guessed it:

that too is wrong. Finally I walked off the field and called the game dumb.

I am still not much better at basketball, but now I no longer think it's a dumb game. I can now enjoy playing as well as watching the game. The difference is, now I know the rules and understand the game. Every game has certain rules that govern them. These rules are what make the game exciting and fun and without them there would actually be chaos and frustration not vice versa.

Many including myself entered marriage the same way I entered my first basketball game. With our emotions in overdrive we fall in love or decide to love someone. Then we get married singing "all we need is love" or "we're gonna make it", only to find ourselves in a whole lot of foul trouble the minute the game begin. We then leave the game or marriage in frustration, or get tossed out in disgust because of foul trouble.

In the game called marriage, love may be the main ingredient or environment in which the game is played but it is not enough. The marriage game has rules. Even Jesus said: *"If you love me keep my commandments"*. I wish I had been told in the beginning that there is definitely more to marriage than love. Then maybe so many of us would not have panicked and sought to jump ship, when the hormone driven, emotionally overloaded feelings we understood or misunderstood as love subsided, or seem to have evaporated in the heat wave of reality called married life.

Though we will examine some later, the focus of this book is not the rules of marriage. I have spoken to too many couples and individuals who have given up. They've surrendered to the enemy's attacks on their marriages, simply because they don't know the value of what they are fighting for. They have no idea who the real enemy is or what are the rules of the game. There are thousands of "how to" books on the market explaining how to build a great marriage. There are also countless marriage counselors providing coaching. Yet so many still choose to walk away. I believe that this is because they lack a reason to fight, and an understanding of the battle they are in.

Many of the reality shows now taking over our television have the same theme. They show people from all walks of life, subjecting themselves or being subjected to extreme conditions, all for the sake of winning something they value greatly, usually large sums of cash. These contestants will endure various forms of deprivation even starvation. They will attempt life threatening acts. Some will eat or subject their bodies to things too gross to mention. They will push and stretch their talents and themselves to new limits. All this and more they do and endure because something they value greatly is on the line.

I am hoping that when the true value of marriage is revealed, more people will be willing to do whatever it takes to fight for and defend their marriage. I am also hoping to stop couples from targeting the wrong enemy, or from fighting each other, by identifying for them the real enemy and revealing his devices and tactics.

In my own life I have honestly found all my answers in Jesus. No kidding. I know it sounds simplistic, so for the purpose of clarity let's start by taking a look at some of the details of my story.

CHAPTER 8

Our Story: Part 1

In December 1991 I married the girl of my dreams a beauty queen from Glassboro State College named Catherine. Three to four days into our honeymoon cruise she was gone to our cabin to be by herself and I was climbing to the highest part of the ship to have a one and one with God.

I needed to find out if I had done something wrong in getting married because how could she get angry with me on our honeymoon. That was my first wakeup call that marriage may not be the love and romance to love and romance fantasy I envisioned. My wife Cathy and I are as different as can be. These are the dynamics.

I grew up in a testosterone factory: a home for boys, with roughly 12 boys. The home was run with strict discipline and structure. We pushed and challenged each other at everything: who's the toughest, the fastest, the strongest, neatest, brightest; who can hold their breath the longest? By the time I was about age ten we were all involved in martial arts (more discipline). Now who's the best fighter? I later attended and graduated from an all boys high school.

To be sensitive or emotional growing up in my world was a sure way to attract much pain, through teasing and fights. I knew little to almost nothing about girls, except for the lies little hormone driven boys tell each other to impress one another. I knew nothing of their emotional and temperamental makeup, never having lived with one. I left the boy's home at age seventeen, and got my legs under me by eighteen with a good job. I was ready to take on the world and find out all that I was missing. Before I could get there however, like Saul on the road to Damascus I was intercepted by Jesus. I surrendered my life totally to Him and never quite got there.

Cathy on the other hand, was raised on an estrogen farm in the country. She is one of 9 siblings: 8 sisters and one brother. Her brother being one of the oldest had left home by the time she came along. She therefore grew up with all sisters. Next, her parents migrated to the United States. That left for the most part the adult or older sisters and a grandmother in charge most of the time. Now let us just say, this did not provide for her the regimental structure and discipline that I grew under in a home for boys.

Her older sisters, being committed Christians did a great job of leading her to Jesus at an early age. She therefore had almost no experience or knowledge of boys, or what men can be like, growing up only with sisters and whatever crazy fantasies they share with each other.

Now, you know God must have an incredible sense of humor when He brought us together, and caused us to fall madly in love with each other. I am pure unadulterated logic and Cathy is emotion times two. A combination like this and you know somebody is going to the crazy house. I saw everything as black or white with a simple explanation for everything. Cathy insisted that there is more to everything than meets the eyes. (By the way, did you know that ladies can be very sensitive and extremely emotional at times?)

Being a man of logic, PMS made absolutely no sense to me and could not be real. (Just something ladies made up to get over on us guys). Now I know better and that it really stands for Praying Men Survive. During that first year of our marriage Cathy demonstrated every side effect on the birth control pill box. (While they were being manifested I had no idea what was the cause). She would get depressed and cry for no apparent reason. I would ask "did I do something" she would say "no." All this for me was maddening and made no sense. My childhood had taught me you should only cry for severe physical pain.

She would call me insensitive and cold, because whenever she would try to explain, it was difficult for me to grasp or sincerely empathize. I would therefore respond by saying dumb things like "well all you need to do is this" or "then if you would just do this or that you would not have this or that problem." How was I supposed to know that she did not want my simple solutions? These just made her feel worse. They only caused her to think that if it is so simple, and she could not figure it out, then she must also be quite stupid.

Our intimate times were exceptionally wonderful. It was the in-between times that were driving us crazy. We were hoping for a smooth ride, the happily ever after fairy tale thingy. Instead we found ourselves on this roller coaster going up today and down tomorrow. Like the song, we found ourselves taking one step forward and two steps back. We were each doing our best, but so often getting it wrong where the other was concerned. The word clueless comes to mind.

Here is a quick example for you. Still within the first eighteen months of our marriage, I came home one day and Cathy who should be home was not. I waited until about 8:00 pm, and still there was no sign of her. I had received no phone call, so getting concerned I started calling around. I shortly found out that she was 60 miles away at her sister's house. She had left no note and had not called. I was ticked off. However, I said to myself: Ainsley, you are not going to blow it this time; you will be sensitive and understanding.

I called and when she came to the phone I asked what I thought were all the right questions.

"Are you all right? Is everything ok? Did I do something wrong? Did I not do something? Why did you just leave without a note?"

She responded by saying it was not any particular thing but rather it was everything; she was just tired of everything and needed a break. She was dizzy from the roller coaster. She had headaches from our constant bumping of heads and emotional welt marks from our rubbing each other wrong. She needed some time. She needed to get off and rest a bit. Trying to be the understanding, sensitive and caring husband I said, "Baby I understand. Sorry things are so crazy. Take as much time as you need." I then went to my room and congratulated myself on how great, sensitive and understanding I was.

The next three days she was there I called her once. Many times I wanted or intended to call her but my logic would overrule my heart by saying to me. "Don't be a jerk! When she said she needed time away, it was not from the house; it was from you. Give her a chance; do not hound her, give her some time!"

On her return three days later she was solemn, withdrawn and obviously upset about something. I pressed her to tell me what was wrong and she did. She asked why I didn't call more often. When I tried to explain my reasons, she explained to me that sometimes a girl likes to be chased or pursued. My not calling made her feel that it did not matter that she'd left. She felt that I did not need her and didn't care.

Now how was I to know she would see it that way? So much for my understanding and sensitivity. We loved each other but our differences kept us off balance and constantly frustrated our efforts to create oneness.

Part 2

When God said it was okay to give up.

Somewhere between 2 to 3 years into our marriage it was my turn to try to get off the roller-coaster. I thought it through, and decided I did not want to spend the rest of my life dealing with these constant ups and downs. I did not want to deal continually with the same things, having to forgive the same wrongs. I concluded if we had not gotten it perfect by then we were never going to get it perfect; therefore, I wanted out.

I did nothing without seeking God's approval, and because from my perspective almost all our problems were my wife's fault, I figured I would explain things to God. I knew He wanted his children to be happy. I knew He would see my point; after all, I did try my best. I whined, griped and complained to God, until He responded to me as clear as I have ever heard God speak into my mind and heart.

He told me to go into thirty, that's three followed by a zero days of fasting. I figured I was not hearing God clearly so I went back. And clearer and probably more certain than I have ever been of the voice of God (not audible), He told me to go into 30 days of fasting.

My reason and logic took over. This made no sense; I had to work. I needed strength. This could hurt me. I went on for days like this not talking to God much, mainly because I did not want to hear what He had to say. Finally, I concluded it did not make sense. I did not want to do it; I couldn't do it and wouldn't do it. After all maybe it was just in my mind.

Right after my decision, the following Sunday in church my pastor stood up and said he believed God was asking him to do something He had never asked him to do before. He said he was totally convinced however, that it was the leading of God and therefore he would obey. He said God told him to put the church on thirty, that's three zero days of fasting. I immediately looked up towards heaven saying: O*h no. You didn't.* Pastor went on to say that this was to be a chain fast. This is when different auxiliaries or groups would begin fasting where another left off until thirty days were accomplished. I was so relieved and happy. I was ready to do seven or so days with the men's group when God spoke into my spirit again more firmly this time saying: "This is not what I desire of you. This is just your confirmation; I now desire that you enter into forty, that's four followed by a zero days of fasting. Afraid He may say fifty next, I immediately agreed.

The next 40 days God changed my marriage, my ministry and my life. As the Lord broke me during this time I understood clearly Isaiah 64:6…**and all our righteousness are as filthy rags.** All this time I saw myself as oh so wonderful, or by the highest standards, still pretty good. God used forty days to adjust my vision, causing me to truly see myself. He showed me that I was often cold and insensitive, also what an unbelievable wretch I was and oh so very far from wonderful.

Regarding my marriage and my desire to call it quits, God told me it was ok. God told me it was perfectly fine with Him for me to give up on Cathy, once I got to that place where I could walk before Him and not need His forgiveness, when I got to that place where it was ok for Him to give up on me for my many failures.

I began to examine my relationship with God and how often I had failed Him. God removed the rose colored glasses through which I saw myself. He revealed to me the way I really was in my relationship with Him. I saw all the times He said don't and I did; He said stop and I kept going; He said do and I didn't, and on and on the slide show of my faults and failures continued. Now in light of this true footage of my relationship with God, with each passing frame my wife grew more incredibly wonderful in my eyes.

Now this is the clincher: In spite of just how horrible I've been towards the God I claim to love with all my heart, He still loved me. I said I loved Him with my lips, but so many times my actions said the opposite. Yet He still loved me.

During this time of consecration and fasting, God caused me to understand the true meaning of unconditional love, the love He has for me, The kind I was to have for my wife. He caused me to know that none of my failures, mess-ups and blunders affected His love for me. He made me to know His love for me was in spite of and not because of me. I began to understand why God's love is called amazing in that while we were his enemies or sinners, Christ who represents the groom died for us who will become his bride.

At the end of forty days of breaking and molding, God had made two things clear about my treatment of, and response to Cathy my wife. First, not only was it my declaration to the world that this is how He, God treated me. It also represented my statement to Him of how I wanted Him to respond and treat me. *And forgive us our debts, as we forgive our debtors.* Matt. 6:12.

When the forty days of fasting was completed God had changed much in me. There was still a lot more growing and changing to come, but I was now able to look at Cathy and sincerely and honestly say to her, "Honey I thank God for you". God had placed a love in me for her at the end of forty days that I could not explain. I was able to say to her, "there is nothing you can or will ever do that will stop me from loving you." At the end of my fast I could honestly say I loved her more than I did when I married her.

Unconditionally is how God loves me and that is what I must model to the world, in my relationship with Cathy. Before the forty days I did not know what I felt for Cathy. I only knew I wanted out of my marriage in a bad way. We were just like many others, trapped, desperate and frustrated ready to move on, until God stepped in and taught me His way.

CHAPTER 9

WHAT EXACTLY DO YOU WANT FROM ME?

Once there was a man in a small town dying from a deadly disease, but the hospital for reasons unknown refused to treat him. As he was dying he called his son to him and said

"Son if you were a doctor I would not have to worry about treatment and probably would not be dying right now."

"That's right papa." The little boy replied.

"Son, I want you to promise me something before I die." The father continued.

"Yes papa, anything papa." His son responded.

"When you grow up and become successful, promise me son that you will treat every patient, that you won't send anyone away, but you will treat everyone; promise me son."

Looking in his father's pleading and dying eyes the son said,

"I promise, I promise you papa I will treat every patient."

After his father died, Radu his son never forgot his promise to his dad. However, by his mid-teens it became clear to Radu that he could never become a doctor. First, he concluded that they were too poor. They could never afford medical school. Secondly, the amount of studying and the number of years it took to become a doctor terrified him. He therefore studied business and decided to go into business for himself. Radu became an overnight success in his business and became very wealthy.

Despite his success Radu was never able to get over his failure to keep the promise he had made to his dying father on his death bed. One day while agonizing over it with his wife, she pointed something out to him. She said, "Honey, you promised your father that you would treat all patients, not necessarily become a doctor. Aren't there other ways to treat patients without being a doctor?"

Radu had never thought of it before, because he knew exactly what his father meant, and what he had promised in his heart, but his wife was right. He had not promised his father that he would become a doctor; he promised to treat all patients. The answer to his dilemma came as quickly at this realization. Radu purchased the little convenience store in the lobby of the hospital and after expanding it he posted a sign. The sign read: "**To All Patients: Present your discharge slip to cashier to receive FREE treat.**"

Radu found peace because finally he was able to keep the promise he had made to his father. Or had he? Radu's father's dying wish and greatest desire was for his son to become a doctor and help the sick. Radu knew this in his heart and had agreed to this. Later however, by carefully examining the phrasing or wording of his promise or commitment, Radu was able to keep his promise, without obeying or doing what his father asked, or becoming what his father desired.

The children of Israel like Radu found a way to obey God's law without truly doing or becoming what God wanted. All the do's and don'ts I learned while studying electronics were not to make me a good keeper of the laws of electronics. The objective of the discipline was to make me an electronic engineer or technician. God had a greater purpose in mind when He gave us the law.

God's instructions to Adam and the things he was made to undergo in the garden were meant to teach and prepare him for something great. Similarly, God's purpose for giving us the laws, ordinances and commandments was not to make us good law keepers. It was to teach us to love, that we might become like Jesus. Jesus explained this with His statement from Matt. 22:36-40.

> *all the laws and prophets are fulfilled in this, love the Lord with all your heart, soul and strength and love your neighbor as yourself.*
> The Apostle Paul stated, *Let this mind be in you Which was also in Christ.* Phil. 2:5.
> Also John said—-*but we know when He shall appear we shall be like Him.* 1John 2:3

Something however went very wrong. The laws focused on the "what to do" and "what not to do". The result was people going through the motions without being changed by the act, and the change is what God wanted in the first place. We have established programs to feed the hungry and assist the needy even though we despise them. We give only because we expect to receive more in return. We worship God not because of who He is or because we believe He is worthy, but because we have been told by someone that this is the way to receive goodies or blessings from God.

The Pharisees were doing everything God commanded yet Jesus called them hypocrites and white washed sepulchers. *Matt. 23:27.* Paul like others of his sect said he was blameless in regards to the law. If they were doing all that God asked and God still found their ways detestable, something had to be wrong somewhere. In deed it was. The problem was not with what they did, but how they did it, and why they did it. Jesus told them that they did things only to be seen of men and they did it without mercy and compassion. These were more important to God than the doing. They had found a way to obey without actually doing or becoming what God wanted.

The apostle Paul therefore, called the law weak in that it had the power to get us to act, but lacked the power to change us. *Rom. 8:3.* We have found a way to do good and remain desperately wicked, with an evil heart and always with a selfish motive.

I remember an incident when I was about thirteen years old and growing up in the boys home. The superintendent had resigned to get married and start his own family. The church, while trying to locate a proper replacement, asked a very prominent and respected lady from the church to fill in temporarily. She said something to us when she arrived that has never left me. She told us that if we thought that what she was doing in accepting the post was because of us, or because she cared anything about us, we were sadly mistaken. She said the only reason she was doing it was because the priest had begged her, and because she wanted to go to heaven.

Jesus came along therefore and changed everything. He not only told us, but also showed us what God wants us to be. Jesus totally removed the emphasis from the "what" and placed it on the "why" and the "how". He broke several of their laws to show that God is more concerned with why we do what we do.

It is a horrible thing to take a knife and cut someone, but if it is done to save someone's life as in a surgery, it is a wonderful thing. It is no longer "thou shall" or "thou shall not" written in stone, but *whatever you do in word or deed do all*...Col. 3:17. Jesus basically told us not to get hung up on the letter of the law because it kills. Embrace instead the spirit and become what God wants. By so doing, we will naturally produce or do what is written in the law, because it is who we are, not something we practice in spite of what we are. In other words, we are not wicked or evil people doing good deeds to score points, but good people being ourselves. See *Matt. 12:35.*

Paul also referred to the law as our schoolmaster. It was meant to prepare us for our profession of loving. We are meant to be trained lovers. Jesus further simplified it for us this way. *A new commandment I give you, love one another as I have loved you.* (John 13:4). The bible says this is what perfection looks like.

Paul, understanding that the focus is no longer what you do, but how you do it and why, wrote the following. He said all things are lawful unto me but all are not expedient or necessary. *1 Cor. 6:12.* Also in 1Cor. 13 he makes it crystal clear, that what you do, regardless how great and wonderful, if it does not flow from the love that is in you because of what you have become, it does not count. Note that in this chapter Paul says, *"And have not love"*, which means to possess love, not just occasionally practice love. It further implies that love has become a part of who you are.

God by changing the focus is ensuring that the Bride of Christ, the Church would not simply go through the motions like Israel, observing the letter while circumventing the spirit of the law. Their emphasis would not be on acting, but on transforming and becoming. *Be ye transformed by the renewing of your mind.* Rom. 12:2.

As in the Garden of Eden Adam underwent many things and was given many instructions but they all served a single purpose. They were to prepare him for his bride and ensure that he loved her unconditionally. So it is with us, we undergo many things and are given many instructions with a single objective in mind. We are being prepared for the Groom (transformed to His image), tested and tried to ensure that we will love unconditionally, even as we are loved. A love we demonstrate through our obedience and commitment to the groom, Jesus Christ, and our love for each other.

1 Corinthians 13:13 says: *and now abides faith hope and charity (love): these three; but the greatest of these is charity (love).* When we see God face to face and know as we are known, and after we've received our reward, there will be no more faith, and no need to hope because they are only needed to embrace the unseen. Only love will last forever.

The truth is this: When all is stripped away, almost every sin and failure in the life of a believer can be narrowed down to a failure to love.

CHAPTER 10

What's My Role?

With the foregone in mind, it must be clearly understood in this next segment that when I speak of the role of the man and the woman in marriage, I speak regarding the "how" and the "why" not the "what". Allow me to explain. When speaking of the "what" in regards to a man's role in marriage, his role is to lead or govern, to provide for and protect his family. **Loving his wife is not the husband's role.** It is the reason and or context in which his role is performed or what I call the "how".

Likewise, **being in submission or in subjection to her husband is not the wife's role in marriage.** This again is the "how" or the context in which her role is performed. According to the bible, her role in the marriage is that of a helper to her husband, a lover and a nurturer by virtue of her design. The role of helper does not refer to being a maid; it's more a picture of the Holy Spirit and the church. She is one who comes alongside to help.

As we pointed out before, you can perform the "what" and still not obey or please God. Just like a husband, a prison will provide for, protect and govern it's inmates also. Therefore, the husband's performance of these responsibilities must be comprised of more than just the act. God has changed the emphasis from the "what" and placed it on the "why" and "how". St. John 3:16 says:

For God so loved the world that He gave His only begotten son, that whosoever believeth in Him should not perish, but have everlasting life. The emphasis is on the "why": "For God so loved."

When you read this next section please note, I too have switched the emphasis from the "what" and placed it on the "how" where it belongs. Whenever I speak of the role of the man or the woman in this portion I refer not to the "what" but to the "how", because that is what really matters.

Whenever two or more people come together to work towards a single objective they are referred to as a team. Marriage therefore can be referred to as a team sport. It is a game where two people work towards achieving the oneness that God intended for married couples to embody and enjoy. The most important ingredient of a successful team is everyone on that team knowing and playing their role well. Regardless of all our other skills and abilities, when we play as a team we must focus, manage, and master the part we are assigned in order for the team to be successful.

Now consider for example soccer, my favorite sport. (Hope you don't hold that against me). Though you may be the greatest goalkeeper in the world, if in a particular game you are assigned the position of striker or center forward, you had better know what this role requires. It will be very hard for your team to win if you keep grabbing the ball with your hands. This will cause your team to be penalized. Neither can you win if you insist on playing defensive instead of attacking: no goals will be scored for your team like this.

A good example of not knowing your role would be this: A friend of mine, on the first time we tried to teach him to play soccer, he kicked the ball into his own goal and began to celebrate. Great is the pain and many are the failed marriages resulting from individuals not knowing the part they play on the marriage team. In a game it is important to know and play your part well. In a marriage it is absolutely vital.

Note the example given us by Jesus. We know that Jesus as His name Emanuel (meaning God with us) implies is fully God. The bible says however that when He was found in the form of man He humbled Himself unto death, even the death on the cross. *Phil. 2:8*. Jesus, though He could do whatever He desired, chose in obedience to fulfill every word and letter that pertained to the role He was playing as the spotless Lamb of God.

The crowd dared Him to come down off the cross if He were really the Son of God. He could have stepped off the cross at any time, but on the cross He was not playing the role of God at that time. He was playing His role as the Lamb of God. (It is amazing what Jesus went through for us yet we find it difficult even to be slightly uncomfortable or inconvenienced for Him).

To couples therefore, if we believe that God is the architect of marriage, we need to check His script before we sign up. We need to understand that we are a small part of a big picture, getting in the game and then trying to change our role will affect much more than we believe. The designer took everything into consideration. There are parts we are called to play that presently we don't understand. When you have an architect, coach or director who is the greatest the world has ever seen, with no close comparison, you don't second-guess him; you trust and obey.

Husbands are called to love their wives as Christ loved the church, and be ready to lay their lives down for them. This is a tough sell to any man. A man would rather be king of his castle, with wives and subjects who are willing to die to protect him. However, when our desire is to create the masterpiece the designer intended, we had better learn our part and stick to the script.

Every man needs to get a clear understanding of the role he is called upon to play in this union. Men are being called upon to play the role of Jesus, in this parallel of Christ and His church called marriage. This realization should serve to make one point unquestionably clear to every husband. He must possess for his wife a self-sacrificing love that is matched by none other.

This love must surpass love for mother, father, children, or twin sibling. This unparalleled love is a nonnegotiable requirement to truly reflect the character of the One we represent. Paul amplifies this for us in Eph.5:28-29:

Wives are called to submit to their husbands. *Eph. 5:22*. Also they are called to be in subjection to their husbands, *1 Peter 3:1* a requirement many women resist and resent. Some just totally reject this. Yet this is a part of the role the architect designed for her in his masterpiece called marriage. Every believer knows that a person cannot be saved without total submission to Jesus Christ. This makes submission a prerequisite and an absolute essential for salvation. It is also one possible reason why Satan fights women in this area seemingly above all others. However, this understanding should underscore for every true woman of God one thing. The absolute necessity their submission to their husband is, for them to be the true reflection and image of the bride of Christ, the role God has chosen for them.

Many times our role involves pain because love sometimes will cause us to hurt very badly. The greater the love the more severe the pain it can cause. Those who don't believe that love can cause pain should read 1Corinthians 13:4, or just ask a woman giving birth to the child she can't wait to hold. Ask a man sustaining injuries on the front line of battle in defense of his family. Better yet, just ask Jesus if the price His love for us made Him pay was painful. When it is over the second question you will ask them is, was it worth it?

Everyone wants the marriage that others admire. Wealth is not the key to this. The fact is statistics show that it can be quite an obstacle. It is obedience to God's Word regarding your respective roles that will ultimately produce for you the peace, joy and happiness your heart desires. It is knowing what God expects of each in our respective roles and mastering it, that will produce the oneness we seek and He intended.

God has promised that His word will not return to Him void or empty but will prosper and accomplish its objective. *Isaiah 55:11*. Bank on it. Jesus said He would erase the heavens and the earth before He allowed one single word of His to fail. Rest assured, if you both follow his script and play your part you will not come up empty.

CHAPTER 11

What's My Motivation?

His

A point that must be made regarding our roles of loving and submitting is this. Act one or the first move belongs to the man. By this I mean that it would be crazy of me or anyone to ask a woman to blindly submit under any circumstance or condition. Not only could this prove to be a fatal mistake in our society, but neither is it biblical. Not according to the script we are suppose to mirror. If the man does not love his wife, he could be demanding that she submits to abusive, degrading and dehumanizing treatment or conditions.

Though this is often done, it is not according to God's script. A man cannot get himself a wife and demand that she submits, simply because he is the head or because he is her husband. God has already demonstrated for us what this approach will produce. When He demonstrated His power and might, and then commanded His people Israel to love Him, it did not work. This caused His people to fear Him, not love Him, which was the objective. A man may use force to get a woman to submit to him for a while. This will get him a maid but not a wife who delights in him. Then the first chance she gets, if she is not too terrified, she will be gone.

Most married men know that if they say or do the wrong thing, at the wrong time, their wife will completely close down emotionally. If he is really clueless, she may even dutifully submit to him sexually, but she remains detached and dead to him. Ultimately, even he will be turned off by this. There is no fulfillment for anyone in this, just heartache and misery. He will eventually say.

"She does what I ask but her heart is far from me. She does not love me."

He eventually responds to her just as God did to Israel in Isaiah 29:13.

The model or pattern marriage is meant to mirror is described in this manner in Rom. 5:8.

But God commendeth his love toward us, in that, while we were yet sinners, Christ died for us.

See also John 4:19.

We love him, because he first loved us.

The bride of Christ, the church is responsive. We respond to love, Christ's love, not because we are loveable or perfect but while we were still sinning, Jesus loved us and demonstrated His love for us in an unquestionable way. We then respond by submitting or surrendering our lives to Him.

This is why I say the first move belongs to the man. For any man to authentically portray his role model, Jesus, he must first demonstrate his unquestionable love for his wife. His demonstration of love will show her that it is safe for her to trust him with her heart, mind and body. It will tell her it is safe to submit and totally surrender. She feels completely secure because he has shown her that he would never knowingly hurt her. He like Christ would be willing to lay down his life to protect her. She comes to understand the meaning of the word *cherished*.

Note this story told about Jesus in Luke 8:19-21.

[19]Then came to him his mother and his brethren, and could not come at him for the press. [20]And it was told him by certain which said, Thy mother and thy brethren stand without, desiring to see thee. [21]And he answered and said unto them, My mother and my brethren are these which hear the word of God, and do it.

Jesus in exacting detail seems to model for us everything He asks of us or expects of us. A man is told to leave father and mother, (the nearest and dearest people to him) and cleave to his wife. In our vows, we promise to forsake all others and cleave to each other, as long as we both shall live. Men should take note that in Jesus' model no person or thing can come before your wife. Your wife is you. You both are made one.

Husbands and wives too must remove or destroy everything that might give someone on the outside an inside track to exert, pull or make demands on them that should be reserved for their spouse alone. The man is called to love his wife as or just like Christ loves the church.

A spouse should never find himself or herself competing with others for the attention and affection that should be theirs, by virtue of their position as wife or husband.

Most men would prefer that the woman they are attracted to first submit and surrender to them, before they declare and overtly demonstrate their love. (It has been said this is because men are insecure and afraid of rejection). I have found that most women will not willingly surrender to any man. However, they will surrender to the love of a man. It is the love to which they surrender, because it is what they are seeking. Everyone has an example of a "how did a guy like that end up with such an incredible girl". The answer is simple: He loved her the way she wanted to be loved and she surrendered to it. It is the men that are said to be visual. Like the church, women are made responsive.

The experts have stated and it is a fact that women use sex to get love and men use love to get sex. What this means is, a man will say and do anything to convince a woman that he loves her, just to have sex with her. It also means that in an effort to get the love she needs, a woman will give her body in the hope that this will make the man love her. The staggering number of single mothers in our society is a telling sign of how many women guessed wrong. The much safer bet is to keep sex where it belongs, within the confines of marriage.

Men I spoke with who called themselves players bragged that they can have any woman. Players are men whose claim to fame is that they've mastered the art of seducing women. Regardless what these so called players look like, they will tell you that a woman will respond. All they need is enough time with her, and the right approach for each. Even though it is pretentious or just an act, they say a woman will respond if she believes she has found true love. She was designed to respond, to submit or surrender to love. One player I know is now happily married to the woman he said was the first he was not able to seduce despite his best moves. She was and is a committed christian and now so is he.

When the bible commands husbands to love their wives, it does more than enable us to reflect the image of Jesus our ultimate objective. It causes the husband to meet his wife's deepest need and desire. It also is the means by which his needs get met.

MARRIAGE...WHY WE FIGHT

The man who fails to love his wife and clearly demonstrate it will create in her a vulnerability that can be exploited by the enemy. At the top of the wife's list of needs is the need to feel valued and accomplished. Because the woman was created for the man, it is extremely important to her that he finds her pleasing. This is why the harsh criticism of a husband is like stab wounds to the heart of a wife. Any criticizing must be done in an atmosphere of love and total acceptance of her.

It is impossible to over emphasize the need for husbands to affirm and reaffirm their wives. When a woman chooses to embrace the role of a wife, deep within, her number one desire and purpose in life is to be a great wife, one pleasing and desirable to her husband. Her husband becomes the only one who is qualified to evaluate her performance in this area. Therefore his lips must compliment her, affirm her, and constantly praise her in this role. For him to say nothing is the same as saying, "What you do as a wife is not worth noting", or "you are failing".

God in His wisdom allowed man in the garden to recognize or discover that there was a great need within. He then created for man a wife to meet or satisfy that need. He brilliantly chose however, to bury deep within the woman what was needed to meet that need in man. God then made the woman a responsive being that will only deliver when loved. This means that for a man to get what he really needs from a woman, he must love it out of her. Trying to force her only causes her to shut down in many different ways.

A man will not have this need met simply by having a woman. It is the woman's response to the man that meets the need within him. The bible tells us in Proverbs 21:9 & 19 that a man will choose to live in the wilderness or in the rafters, rather than in a sprawling mansion with a woman that is not responding to him correctly.

A woman should know that while her beauty will attract a man, (because men are visual), it will not keep him. It is her response to him that keeps him. This is why God in His wisdom made her responsive. God commands the husband to love his wife because it meets her greatest needs, her need to feel secure, cherished, valued and desirable. When He commands wives to honor their husbands, submit to and be in subjection to their husbands, He had a very good reason for this too.

Hers

When God created man He placed within him certain needs and desires, just like He placed in the salmon the need to return to the place of its spawning to lay eggs and die. Certain birds will travel thousands of miles to an exact location for or during a certain time or season. Scientists aren't sure why or how some creatures do these strange things. They just know they do or die trying. There is a similar drive, a need or an innate desire that God has placed in the man also. This is the need and desire to conquer, to rule or to be head.

In Genesis chapter 1 we see God declaring that He would make man in His image. He said they would be made to have dominion over, rule, conquer, and subdue everything on the planet. Knowing now just how disobedient and rebellious we can be, had God not placed something in us to accomplish this we might have chosen to just sit around like the lion and do nothing except hunt, kill, eat and sleep.

Evident also from the way the family was set up, by virtue of the fact that man was made first and woman then made from him, God by design made him head of his family. This headship was not the master servant kind we see today. It was rather the kind Jesus describes in Luke 22:25-27 and Mark 10:42-45. In regards to his wife, the kind of headship God intended is the kind modeled by Jesus, the ultimate Lord and ruler. It was a servant leadership. This as explained earlier was to exist in a context of pure selfless, self-sacrificing love.

This should have resulted in the woman and the man ruling the rest of creation together, even as we will some day reign over the earth with Christ as joint heirs. Always keep in mind that we are the reflection of something far greater.

Please observe carefully that when Jesus returns from the marriage supper or honeymoon with His bride He does not return with her to reign over her. They return to reign together as indicated in Rev. 20:4.

When sin entered the picture in Eden, this team leadership arrangement changed. God then told the woman that the man would now rule over her and her desire would be toward him. Since then we have seen throughout the world in almost every culture and even most religions that men rule over women including their wife or wives. Men subjugate and dominate women by force and most cultures even have laws to ensure that their status never changes. They are treated in some places like animals and worse. This is not what God intended.

Men now seek to rule over women from a standpoint of selfish lust instead of a standpoint of selfless love. This was never God's design or intent as Jesus explained and demonstrated. It is the result of sin. In our sin dominated world men will subdue women and conquer them like anything else. In an effort to satisfy the urge or need within and just as God said she would, the woman still desires him.

There are many things about men that are linked to this innate need to conquer and rule that women seem totally unable to understand. Men can't even explain some of the affinities and urges that drive them. From infancy to old age boys and men compete in everything. You can trust me on this one: I grew up in a boy's home.

Men compete in everything, not just the usual sports and gambling. They will go from the trivial to the disgusting to the deadly: who can burp the longest, spit the farthest, eat the most, drive the fastest, consume the most alcohol, do more or deadlier drugs and who is daring enough to do the most asinine and dangerous stunt or prank. Men love any kind of challenge, for some the more violent the better. Women will watch a group of men watching a game and be totally baffled at how engrossed and passionate they can become.

This has nothing to do with socioeconomics, nor is it cultural. Every place on the planet where men exist the struggle for supremacy also exists. The fact is the first murder committed was the result of sibling rivalry between brothers. *Gen. 4:3-8.* It is not taught. It is just there.

Some men are totally powerless against the woman who understands this God implanted need in man and how to use it to her advantage. *Prov. 7.* Thrones have been abandoned and empires brought down, by women who understood the ego in man. Delilah spoke to Samson about his great strength: a man's favorite subject. By daybreak he was bald, blind, and behind bars.

On the flip side we read this in Proverbs 31:10

Who can find a virtuous woman? for her price is far above rubies.

[11]*The heart of her husband doth safely trust in her,* ***so that he shall have no need of spoil.***

[12]*She will do him good and not evil all the days of her life.*

Proverbs 31:30 refers to her as the woman that fears the Lord. Spoil or spoils are not just wealth or treasures acquired from the enemy after a victory in battle. To a man spoils are also the trophies of war, the symbols of his triumphs and conquests. It is why the hunter stuffs and mounts his kill. It is not enough that he knows; he must prove to everyone else also. His spoils tell the world that he is the best, that he won. This is the heart's cry of every man: "That the world may know that he is the best or among the best". Note carefully that this woman's husband does not have need for spoil.

By obeying God this wife is able to meet the innermost need of her husband. He therefore has no need to go about constantly trying to prove himself. He has no need to beat his chest in public and declare: "I am the man". There is someone at home who does it for him. He is confirmed and reaffirmed as head, as champion, and king of his castle, by the way his wife and kids respond to him. He has no need of spoils.

Much of what a man does is aimed at impressing women. The wise woman is one who understands this and who is able to convince her husband how totally impressed she already is with him. She is able to motivate him in his area of weakness, without ever making him feel weak. He therefore has no need to go out and secure spoils to prove his greatness, his worth or his value. She has created a confident man who will embrace any challenge and fight any battle because of the help and empowerment of his wife.

The husband that does not have this need for respect met by his wife is constantly trying to prove himself. Because it is a need, if he does not find it at home he will look elsewhere for it. He becomes easy prey for the skilled seductress. Yet the man or woman who really fears the Lord shall escape.

God analyzed Adam's needs in the garden. He then carefully formed Eve to embody that which was needed to meet and satisfy those needs and longings inside of Adam. Marriage is referred to as settling down because the restless yearnings and longings of both should be satisfied by each other when it is done God's way and functions according to His rules.

When we establish our marriage relationships according to God's word, when we treat and respond to each other exactly as God said, we will have need of nothing emotionally or psychologically. We will create oneness and completeness in each other. When husbands love their wives as Christ loves the church she is secure and immune to a "player's" best approach because she already has true love and is totally satisfied.

When the wife submits to, honors, and obeys her husband she makes him feel like a king, and therefore he has nothing left to prove to anyone. Whenever he wants to feel great about himself he simply goes home. His lips should and will constantly praise her. She makes him immune to the flattery of the seductress because he already knows he is "all that". We not only complete each other when we do it God's way, we also secure our borders and affair-proof our marriages.

At this point, based on how God has designed marriage to function it should be obvious what the number one destroyer of marriage would be. You guessed it, selfishness. It is always right there leading the charge in every failed marriage.

God's wisdom is mind blowing, isn't it? God has created us and established marriage in such a way, that the only way for each person to receive what he or she desperately needs and desires is by striving to meet the needs of his or her spouse. This proves once again that we are the biggest losers when we choose to disobey God.

Similarly, mankind's deepest needs can never be met apart from our obedience to God. When we love, submit, and serve Him as we should, then the longings, hunger and desperations within our hearts and souls get met or satisfied by God, because

He delights in us. 'Seek ye first the kingdom of God and His righteousness' all else gets added after. *Matt.6:33.*

This further helps us to understand why the bible declares things like,

'...*it is more blessed to give than to receive*' **Acts 2:35.** *"Give and it shall be given unto you good measure pressed down and shaken together..."* **Luke 6:38.** *"...do to others what you would want them to do to you."* **Matt. 7:12 (NIV)** *None of you should look out just for your own good. You should also look out for the good of others.* **Phill. 2:4 (TNIV).** *"Esteem others more highly than yourself."* **Phil. 2:3,** and *Be kindly affectionate one to another."* God's way really works.

CHAPTER 12

You Know I Love You, Don't You?

Every person has a love language. This is that act that when done to or for that individual, communicates to that person (in a way they understand or can relate to) that the doer truly loves them. Examples of love languages are, giving of gifts, words of affirmation, touch or acts of kindness. Some people have multiple love languages. My wife Cathy's love language includes words of affirmation, touch and gifts and definitely flowers. Mine is without doubt acts of kindness. I've said many times to her: *"Do not tell me show me.*

Jesus also has a love language and if we are to be His bride we had better learn it. His love language may seem strange, and so He told us clearly what it is:

St. John 14:15 *If ye love me, keep my commandments.*

He then goes on to say in John 13:4.

A new commandment I give unto you, that ye love one another; as I have loved you, that ye also love one another.

This is Jesus' only love language, and he made it clear with statements like Matt. 5:23 & 24, where He said: if you are bringing a gift to the altar, and remember there is a problem between you and your brother, do not bother giving the gift until you have first gone and made it right between you and your brother. He further went on to say in Matt. 25:40,

Verily I say unto you, Inasmuch as ye have done it unto one of the least of these my brethren, ye have done it unto me.

Jesus makes it crystal clear that the only way to love Him or express our love for Him is to love and express it to one another.

How important is mastering the love language of our spouse? It is so important that Jesus said of His love language that if you don't speak or master it He will not marry you. *John 15:12 and Matt. 7:21-23.* Many times couples are trying their best, but end up frustrated because it seems their partners just don't get it. Most of the time there is a simple reason for this. They are speaking their own love language not their spouse's.

Consider this: I speak only Spanish. You are trying to convince me on the phone that you love me and want to marry me. Though you speak seven different languages, if one of them is not Spanish you will never convince me. Regardless of how many times you call me, my answer will be the same because I only understand Spanish. I will therefore probably respond something like "Tienen el numero equivocado" (You have the wrong number) and hang up.

In 1Cor.13 1-3 God's word tells us that many people are trying to speak to him but they are speaking their own language instead of His. To win Him over we speak in tongues, we prophesy, reveal mysteries, do great acts of faith and give extremely generously. We still fall short however if we have not learned to master the only romance language Jesus understands. He will think you don't love Him and only want to move into His house. He will see all our effort as a cheap pick up, and will respond in the end "depart from me I do not know you". Let us not forget that the celebration in heaven is a marriage supper.

The above may appear as if I am advocating salvation by works. I am not. Salvation is by grace through faith alone. Faith however is the visible acts that manifest, demonstrate or make evident the invisible beliefs we hold within.

MARRIAGE...WHY WE FIGHT

Just like we are able to say 'I love you' in many ways without actually saying the words, we can say the opposite also without actually saying it. While we must allow our spouses to be themselves, we must be mindful and make special accommodations for each other's handicaps. In the same way special adjustments and modifications are made in a home to accommodate a person with certain physical handicap, so too must we make adjustments in our behavior to accommodate an emotionally handicapped spouse. If your spouse is from divorced parents, was raped, molested, abused or is a divorcee, he or she usually carries deep scars, wounds or what I refer to as emotional handicaps.

The bible instructs husbands in 1 Peter 3:7 to live with their wives according to knowledge, giving honor to them as the weaker vessel. This is actually a two way street. It means we ought to be mindful of the limitations within each other. Then with that knowledge or 'According to knowledge' we should then make the necessary adjustments and honor our spouse despite whatever their limitations.

Based on our past or our upbringing we may all respond to the same thing differently. For example, what may be a desired or preferred sexual advance for most, maybe a turn off and even traumatic for a spouse who was a rape victim. Adjustment would have to be made in this area to accommodate a spouse with this emotional handicap. It is important to know your spouse and know how certain things affect them; know what certain actions say to them. You may have grown up in a home where a slap on the rear is a great sign of affection. To a severely abused spouse however, a raised hand or a slap of any kind may send a much different message. You will just have to become more creative. (Lots of hugging and cuddling suggested).

Thomas, one of Jesus' disciples had a problem in the area of faith or believing though many others did not. Jesus made special accommodations for his doubt, by having him put his finger in the nail wound and his hand in the spear wound in His side. *John 20:24-27.* This may seem extreme or gross to you or me, but this is what love does. It adjusts to accommodate our shortcomings.

We will not make certain jokes. We will avoid certain places. We will refrain from certain actions and we will not have some things in our home. These are some of the things we may have to do, because of the emotions they conjure or the damaging impact they have on our spouse's wellbeing. This is what love does. In Romans 14 Paul puts it this way: though you love meat if it causes your brother to stumble adjust and become a vegetarian while he is around for his sake. How much more your wife or husband? This is what love does.

The entire plan of salvation is about God adjusting to our handicap called sin, so that we may be able to enter his house. Paul refers to the person bothered by certain things as weak in faith. So whether this weaker vessel is the wife or the husband, we honor them and accommodate them, because this is what love does. *Rom. 14.*

CHAPTER 13

Some scary stuff

God does not hold us to a standard higher than His own. In the Old Testament we see God referring to the nation of Israel as His bride. We then see God (in Jer. 3:8) writes them a bill of divorce because of their adultery.

Now Jesus has chosen for himself a bride, the church. By this I am not saying that Jews are excluded because the church started with Jews only. Though there will be millions of Jews in the bride of Christ; the nation as a people is not the bride. God has established new criteria apart from nationality, that all must meet to qualify to be in the bride of Christ. *Matt. 8:11-12.*

Jesus in St. Matt. 19:9 said, *"Whosoever shall put away his wife, except it be for fornication, and shall marry another, committeth adultery."*

Here Jesus gives sexual immorality as the only grounds under which God will undo what He does in the marriage ceremony. The clause "except it be for fornication" indicates an exemption to the no divorce allowed rule. Therefore, if there is fornication / adultery involved, God will honor, recognize or allow the offended to divorce or put away the offender. This in turn means that God who first joined them has released this individual. If they are freed by God, it would also imply that there is no adultery being committed if the offended remarries. However, divorce is not automatic.

The understanding here it that the people who commit adultery not only sin against their own souls, they also give their spouses the power, to have God undo what He did when He joined them as one. Repentance, forgiveness and reconciliation are preferable, highly recommended and encouraged. But the God given right to separate cannot be denied the individual who chooses it in the case of adultery. Jesus always has the final word.

(Now I am aware that through the Apostle Paul, the bible also gives abandonment by an unsaved spouse as grounds for divorce, here again the divorcee is not under bondage. Like Paul most Pastors have encountered specific situations apart from that given by Jesus, where they may personally believe a divorce is justified. Fortunately we are not allowed to add to God's final word which the bible represents. Also, if all those specific situations were listed as grounds for divorce, there would not be a single unjustifiably or unbiblical divorce, because everyone would find a way to make their situation fit. The aim should not be discovering ways to escape your marriage, but rather rediscovering its inventor's or God's original design, desire and intent for marriage. Also, how and why you need to fight to make it a reality in yours).

I must make emphatically clear the destructive power of adultery in marriages to every couple that sits before me for counseling. There is just too much at stake, too much to lose, much too much heartache and pain involved. It is a deadly poison that kills slowly and painfully. DO NOT MESS WITH IT.

There is a reason why God did not want the children of Israel living together with the sinful people of the lands they were to possess. Every addict and many who have fallen into sin will tell you that there is a point where sin takes control. This is the place where the will fails and desire, greed, and lust reign supreme.

Anyone familiar with wood or coal fires knows that if you stoke or fan a dying or smoldering fire long enough it will soon become a blaze. If you keep feeding it, it will soon enough destroy everything around.

Our sinful nature is always with us. In the book of Romans, chapters 6 and 7, Paul gives us a graphic picture of the battle we all fight to conquer this sinful nature within us all. God knows that being constantly exposed to sin will accomplish two things in us. It will stoke the fires of our own sinful desires. Also, it will desensitize us to how evil or wicked our sins are. Certain sins have become accepted norms.

There is no such thing as innocent flirting. This is where most adulterous relationships begin. It is just our way of testing the waters, to see if we still have it. THAT'S FIRE YOU'RE PLAYING WITH. Someone will get burnt, even if the flirter is only playing. Most of the time in our sex crazed society the recipient of the advances will take it seriously; and if heartbreak does not occur something worse will.

Many who have thought flirting to be innocent have learnt otherwise. In our society where sex is used to sell even water, they have watched as much of what they have labored for, go up in the smoke of a sexual harassment lawsuit. IS IT WORTH IT?

There are certain doors that a married person should never open when dealing with the opposite sex. We will always begin where we left off. This means, once you have told someone how you feel about them and your desires for them they cannot unknow it. From that point forward your every action will be filtered through this knowledge. Even innocent interactions thereafter will be interpreted as expressions of a desire to get to the next level or through the next door. Once certain doors have been opened in a relationship our awareness will make it impossible to close. These doors will lead to a place where sin rules.

Any verbal expression of desire, love, or sexual attraction to anyone other than your spouse, even in jest is a door opened that cannot be shut. There* is a fire out of control. Almost any physical contact after this point and your house is on fire. Your only way to survive at this point is to do as the bible says in 2 Timothy 2:22. You run away like Joseph did in Geneses 39:12 and never look back. (Run away from the source of temptation and not your spouse).

If you choose not to run, believing that you are in control, like the drug addict, alcoholic, or addicted gambler, you will watch your will take a back seat to your desires. You will watch as sin takes over, causing fires to burn out of control, threatening everything you hold dear or until there is nothing left but ashes.

Always keep the home fires burning, and never expose your flame to certain fuel. What you think will warm you can explode, destroying everything you treasure. KEEP THE DOORS CLOSED AND LOCKED.

Pornography is one of the devil's favorite means of corrupting us. STAY AWAY. An adult, especially a married person playing with pornography is like a baby playing with a loaded gun. Sooner or later both of them or someone close to either one will die or be seriously injured. Only in the case of the adult it is a lot worse. There are serial killers on death row that will confirm this. An adult playing with pornography will do more than cause physical death. It will cause emotional and psychological death; it kills relationships, marriages and families. It robs innocence, and leaves gaping wounds upon the heart, mind and soul. DON'T EVEN THINK ABOUT IT.

King David, God's righteous servant murdered an innocent man after committing adultery with the man's wife. This came about because he went to a peep show on his roof and watched a woman bathing. BE AFRAID. Pornography can keep killing long after the initial exposure.

Jesus also said that whosoever looks on a woman to lust after her has already sinned. (*Matt. 5:28*). This may sound extreme, but the danger is really that great. There is nothing innocent about pornography. BE VERY AFRAID.

What about gay marriages and such?

You knew I was going to get here eventually, didn't you? Here is my simplest response. In every Christian marriage ceremony, there is a very important disclaimer that should always be issued by the minister, before he performs the ceremony. It goes something like this, "BE WELL ASSURED THAT IF ANY PERSONS ARE JOINED TOGETHER OTHER THAN GOD'S WORD ALLOWS THEIR MARRIAGE IS NOT LAWFUL." This means God will only unite and join what He has approved and that is a man and a woman. Jesus clearly stated in Mark 10:6 that the inventor of marriage, God, created a male and female for the purpose of marriage.

It is unthinkable and mind boggling to me, that any minister or servant of God could endorse an abomination to God, such as homosexuality, then present it before God to be blessed by Him. Understand carefully, I am not referring to homosexuals as abominations. They are just sinners like the liar, thief, fornicator or murderer, and all of us fit multiple categories before we came to know Jesus as our Lord and repented. All sinners, including those practicing homosexuality are welcome in the house of God. This is not, however, to have their sinful lifestyles endorsed by the church or blessed by God.

Homosexuals too, like the liar, thief, or murderer must turn from their sinful ways or repent, to be acceptable to God. How could anyone, having read Genesis 19, Leviticus 20:13 or Romans 1:27 then take two people practicing this sin before a holy God and ask Him to bless their sin. Homosexuals should not be treated differently from any other open sinner in God's Church. We are not allowed to discriminate. Christians cannot hate them or treat them like lepers and expect them to repent and come to Christ. No one wants to be where they are hated. As Christ's representative, we'll reach them the same way we reach any other sinner: We love them in.

Mankind and society can endorse whatever they please. The church or body of Christ cannot. What if a serial killer or a career criminal came into the church one day? They say to the pastor: "Sir I am a serial killer. I enjoy killing people. This is the only thing that brings me joy and fulfillment." The thief says, "Sir I am a thief; robbing people makes me feel good about myself. It gives me joy and happiness. Sir we want you to pray for us that God would bless us and prosper us in these our chosen professions. We've come that you might ask God to sanctify us, cover us, and grant us much success as we continue to murder and steal."

Everyone including this pastor would be outraged, shocked and appalled at the presumptuous irreverence. They would be called names like 'unrepentant reprobates', 'without a moral compass or conscience'. Why then are there organizations calling themselves churches endorsing the sin of homosexuality and asking God to bless it, while many members smile, nod and say amen?

Now I know this is where I get accused of equating homosexuals with mass murderers and criminals. Well, no, they are not the same. The fact is some of the nicest people you know could be homosexuals. However, consider this. Several years ago a police officer stopped a minister and drugs were found in his car. Though he protested that they were not his, he was tried and sentenced. He had to spend some time in prison. He was thrown in the same prison with rapists, murderers, thieves and child molesters, though no one would accuse him of being the same as they. The minister got no special treatment in the court of law, and without repentance neither will sinners get special treatment in God's courts. God does not bless our abominable acts; He will not go back on His word.

Homosexuals like any other willful sinner with unholy passions and sinful habits, must be told that they need to repent, which means turning from and renouncing their sinful lifestyles or they will go to hell. Putting a saddle on a pig, regardless how cute it looks, does not make it a horse. It is okay to embrace the sinner, but we must emphatically reprove sin. Sin is not sin contingent on who does it. Sin is sin because God says it is.

I find it funny that some in our courts and governments are sanctioning homosexual unions and calling them marriages. Funny, because lets say I made a painting of a woman in my basement. I then tried to market it as the Mona Lisa. This same court would send me to prison for fraud. Let's say I create identical replicas of the twenty-dollar bill and begin to spend them. This same court would send me to prison for counterfeiting, because they or a duly recognized authority did not make it.

How then can this same court take the recognized God-ordained institution of marriage and gut it of all that God meant it to be? They then market it as a contract between any two persons for the purpose of securing economic, social and legal benefits and privileges. Let's face it, the courts did not create or invent marriage. They simply recognize it and choose to honor it. If they choose not to honor it with special privileges that is fine. But they do not have the right to tamper with God's masterpiece, not without a resounding cry of righteous indignant outrage from God's people, the Church.

The bottom line is, God does the joining in marriage and He will only join according as His Word allows. His Word clearly does not allow for two men or two women. It does not allow a man and his dog, a woman and her cat or a farmer and his horse. His Word does not allow marriage to under age children, and if you leave a husband in Texas and are trying to be joined to another in New Jersey He will not join you either. We call that bigamy. He calls it adultery.

Therefore, if you are not a single man and a single woman standing before God, He will not join you, though a dozen bishops, two priests and a rabbi performed your ceremony. You will leave the same way you entered as far as God is concerned, though the entire world may recognize you otherwise. In the final analysis, God's opinion is the only opinion that counts.

Regardless of how our societies or we feel about the truth, the church's responsibility does not change. The church has been called by God to represent God. It cannot therefore have an agenda apart from God's purpose. The church leadership is instructed in scripture to preach God's Word in season and out of season. It is to be declared whether people will hear or not. *2Tim. 4:1-4 and Ezek. 2:7.* As faithful stewards our objective is biblical accuracy and faithfulness, not political correctness.

Now that we have identified institutions and forces that threaten marriages, we have an idea of some of what we should attack, and what to stay away from. We've also figured out that Satan is most likely behind the attacks, but why and what exactly is he up to?

CHAPTER 14

Satan's Mission

From before the dawn of creation Satan's mission has been and remains the same. Satan is a liar and a thief. He was thrown out of heaven because he tried to steal God's glory. Man was made to have dominion or rule over the earth. When Satan got here the first thing he did was lie and deceived man into disobedience and stole lordship of the earth from man. His desire (as the bible said) is to be like God. Everything therefore that belongs to God he wants to either steal or destroy, because of his envy and hatred of God. Satan may use different approaches and strategies but his objective has remained the same: steal what belongs to God and destroy whatever he can't have; beginning with what is nearest and dearest to God's heart.

Beginning in the Garden of Eden we see him targeting the woman. The question is however, targeting her for what? The answer is death. Satan's objective was not simply to get man to rebel against God; his objective was to kill Adam's wife. How so, you ask? Good question. Let us examine the facts.

Satan is evil, not stupid. He knew that God created all things by the power of His Word. He also knew therefore that once God had spoken the Word, God had to do nothing else, because God's Word had in it the power to accomplish all by itself. (*Isaiah 55:11*). He therefore knew just like Adam did that it was totally irrelevant that the fruit would open their eyes and make them smarter, because unlike him God did not lie and Eve was most certainly going to die. He therefore set out to kill Eve by having her ignorantly commit suicide by disobeying God. (How many Christians do you know that satan has taken out this very same way, having them destroy themselves with the things their hearts desire, crave and lust after?). Guard your heart.

Satan's mission from the beginning was to kill the woman. Without the woman there is no marriage, no children or continuance of the race. His mission has not changed from Genesis to Revelation. His mission has been to destroy the woman, or that which is represented by her. *Rev. 12.*

Since Adam voluntarily chose to follow Eve, this means that she was his target. We can see this consistency throughout scripture. When God chose Israel as His people referring to them as His bride, (*Jer. 3:8*), satan targeted them like no other people on earth. They were targeted for not just subjugation but for annihilation. The Pharaoh's attempt to kill all the male children of the Israelites was one sure way of wiping out the race. Since then we have seen many others come along with the exact same agenda. We have seen the likes of Antiochus, Hitler, the KKK, and Islamic extremists attempt to wipe them off the face of the planet.

Next, we see Eve's ultimate representation, the church, the bride of Christ, we who are the sons of God and joint heirs with Jesus. *John 1:12, 1John 3:1, Romans 8:14 & 19.* Being true to form, we see Satan targeting the church for destruction. In the whole Garden of Eden experience God wanted to give us a true representation of what was to come. God was revealing to us not just His purpose but also satan's intent. Understanding therefore that Eve symbolizes or represents the church, it should now be clear what Satan's true purpose and mission is.

God was revealing to us that Satan would go after the church to kill and destroy us by having us violate God's Word which is already established. Jesus also reiterated satan's purpose with His statement in John10:10.

The thief cometh not, but for to steal, and to kill, and to destroy: I am come that they might have life, and that they might have it more abundantly.

The church has been given many titles, and is referred to in many different ways. Our true identity is revealed in God's word however and that is, we are the true sons of God. *John 1:12, 1John 3:1 and Romans 8:14 & 19.* When we lay aside the typologies, shadows and symbolic references to the church, it then becomes clear, that Satan's true targets are and have always been the sons of God. Satan was jealous of God's glory. The bible tells us that Satan's desire was to elevate his throne above God's and be worshiped as God. *Isaiah 14:13—14.* He therefore tried to overthrow God.

We the church or saints, are told in Galatians 4:5-7 that we've been adopted by God and made joint heirs with Jesus. We've been promised that we will be given crowns and shall reign with Christ. The very thing that Satan coveted and fought to steal from God, we are being freely given by God. Can you now begin to imagine the impact this revelation would have on an envious, self absorbed being that is full of pride?

Men, who were created lower than the angels, will be elevated above angels, as God's children to reign with Him. Satan's pride cannot allow this. Therefore, he has set out to kill every child of God in an effort to steal their inheritance. If Satan did not want God above him, imagine how he feels about us who were beneath him being raised above him. However,

God's word made it clear that neither the world nor Satan had any idea, who were the true sons of God. *Rom. 8:19-23.* Therefore from Eve to Israel he has targeted any and everyone he believed might fit the role, but kept guessing wrong.

Then Jesus came and narrowed the field. Thus Romans 8:16 and Eph. 1:13-14 state that the Holy Spirit, who is the earnest or down payment of our inheritance now identifies us as the sons of God. Satan therefore has declared all out war on us. Christians have been fed to lions, boiled in oil, burnt at the stake, stoned to death, starved out, shot, bombed, beheaded and imprisoned to name a few of his methods. All this and more was done to them only because they were Christians.

To the same unimaginable extent that God loves us, Satan's hatred for us is just as passionate and intense. With his track record, why we choose to follow him I'll never know.

Marriage is to God a token, a symbolic reminder of His love and intent to deliver us and glorify us. To us marriage is a symbol of hope, the cornerstone of civilization. To Satan marriage is like salt in his wound, pepper in his eyes, or cold air on his cavity, (if he has any). He hates marriage and for good reason from where he stands. He loathes and despises it and will never rest until he is able to destroy it from the earth if he is permitted. My question is: <u>Will we let him?</u>

CHAPTER 15

How will he do it?

Satan is a big subscriber to the old adage, "if it's not broken, don't fix it". Satan will use what he has always used, that which has worked for him from the beginning. He will use lies and deception. This is why he is called the deceiver of the brethren, the father of lies and a liar from the start. *John 8:44.* Through deception he was able to convince Eve that she would not die, tricking her into rebelling against God and doing what God told her not to do. Satan got her to believe that her heart's desires and dreams would be met by eating of the forbidden fruit. He convinced her that God was not being truthful. In one stroke of genius Satan was able to steal everything from man. He stole our birthright, robbed us of paradise, our fellowship with God, the harmony between man and woman, our health, our righteousness and innocence.

God again did not leave us to guess as to what Satan's approach might be. Rather, He gave us a crystal clear picture of him and his method. Satan has and will remain true to form, to the script or the word of God. Satan will destroy marriage the same way he has destroyed everything else that he hates. He will destroy it through deceptions and lies.

Satan has been able to have us smoke cigarettes even as we watch our friends die from smoke induced lung cancer, and so many other smoke related diseases. He's been able to convince us that it can never happen to us. He has many strung out on drugs because they were sure they would not get hooked, or that trying it once wouldn't hurt. Lies.

The bible tells us that all liars shall have their special VIP reserved spot in the lake of fire. *Rev .21:8*. Satan got us started by telling us that if no one gets hurt there is no harm in lying. Now we are lying so much that we are totally unable to recognize truth. Jesus said that He is the truth. He also said that: You shall know the truth and the truth shall make you free; *John 8:32* and again seek and you shall find. *Matt. 7:7*. Satan has impoverished and imprisoned us through deceptions and lies. Then to ensure that we never break free by discovering the truth (Jesus Christ), he now declares truth to be relative and thus unknowable. Lie.

He now has us believing that everybody is right, that each of us has our personal truth that is only right for us, and therefore need not seek for or listen to anyone else's truth. Look now at the sheer genius of Satan's lies. God's word says we are born in sin and shaped in iniquity, *Ps. 51:5* also there is a way that seems right unto a man but the end thereof are the ways of death. *Prov.16:25*. If this is true, and it is, then Satan was able to secure reserved seating in hell for all who bought his lies about truth and do nothing to find truth (Jesus), because they supposedly already have their own truth.

Examine the power of one lie. God's word says, sex outside of wedlock is wrong and will cost us paradise. Satan says, "Not so! God doesn't want you to have any fun and experience love." We buy this lie and we party on as millions die from AIDS. Multitudes die of other debilitating, incurable Sexually Transmitted Diseases (STDs). This continues while our society drowns in an overwhelming flood of pornography and sexual depravity that debases us all. We party on and enjoy the so-called love that Satan promises, as suicide rate skyrockets and depression cripples the minds, souls and bodies of its victims. We build larger prisons to house the fruits of our sex-without commitment relationships. Society has gotten tired of dealing with these fatherless children. Satan then offers the solution.

The bible calls children a gift from God. *Psalm 127:3*. Satan however was able to convince us that in our sex-crazed society they are nothing more than unwanted inconveniences, a bother, and a burden. After we bought into that lie, he went further. He said that they aren't even human until after they are born. He said, "I'll tell you what they are; they are just fetuses, yeah, that's right, mere blobs of tissue, a simple pile of nothing. I say you should get rid of it before it becomes human."

We thought about it briefly, thought about our life styles and lusts and said to Satan, "that's right." We therefore build abortion clinics to murder our own offspring. Satan was able to deceive us into killing our own helpless young.

You can see Satan being true to form, as he sets his sights on marriage. He has made us rethink everything that God has said marriage should be. It is no longer permanent or until death, but rather until we've had enough. No longer is the man the head of his household. It's now 50/50 at best or whoever makes more money calls the shots. As we embrace more of his subtle changes he gets closer to his goal of destroying marriage.

The clincher that he is up to his same old twisted, subverting, lying, deception can be clearly seen with his latest declaration: That is, "we need to redefine marriage." The bible calls Satan subtle because of his approach. This redefinition has not just sprung from out of nowhere. Rather it has been many years in the making. Examine his slick pattern of subverting truth and deceiving us into embracing lies as he coaxes us towards our own destruction.

- He convinced us that we do not need to be married to be sexually active.
- Marriage is not permanent: divorce should be on demand.
- Sex does not have to be between male and female.
- Homosexuality is not wrong.
- Not only is homosexuality not wrong, it's a beautiful, equal, morally sound alternative to heterosexuality.
- If they are equal, heterosexuals should not enjoy special privileges through marriage?
- Marriage is not special, just another legal contract.
- Homosexuals should be allowed to marry and marriage should be redefined.

Whatever you think of Satan you must give him this, he is very good at what he does.

Though I believe that Satan would like nothing better, and will surely try, he will not succeed in wiping marriage off the planet. The bible says that in the last days as in the days of Noah, before Jesus comes, many will be marrying and given in marriage. It goes on to say they will be lovers of pleasure more than lovers of God. Satan's plan is more sinister. Satan is a corrupter. He didn't kill Eve. He got her to corrupt herself. He was not trying to kill Job but rather he was trying to get him to corrupt himself or curse God. By trying to get Jesus to forgo his purpose, come down from the cross or hate us, Satan's aim was to corrupt Him in order to own Him. Do not forget that it is sin that produces death.

To destroy a masterpiece it is not necessary to burn or crush it. All you need to do is alter it. Several years ago I worked in the home of a very wealthy gentleman who was a collector of very rare and expensive artifacts. As we worked throughout this mansion the custodian told us that if anything needed to be moved we should notify him and he would do the moving or instruct us accordingly. As I wired a sitting room I noticed a plain looking old wooden chair and an old dresser against a wall. Portions of the front edge of the chair were worn as thin as a dull knife. I commented to the custodian that a lot of bottoms must have slid from that chair. He laughed.

Next, I pointed out a very prominent break in one end of the dresser and began telling him how he could have it fixed to look like new. He laughed again then went to the library in the next room and returned shortly with a book. He opened the book and showed me the exact dresser with the exact break in it in the book. He then told me of the master craftsman who built the dresser over 200 years ago for some king and how it got broken. He further explained that the piece was worth millions of dollars, but if that break were ever repaired it would be worthless. All I need to destroy the Mona Lisa is a paintbrush and some paint to fix what I think is wrong with it.

Satan has convinced us that marriage as God designed it has problems. It therefore needs fixing or redefining. What he will have us fix however is the very thing that gives it its meaning and value to God. What we must understand about Satan is that he has limited power. We see this in Job 1 when he had to get permission from God to touch Job. He is not able to do to us what he wants. His best weapon therefore is getting us to violate God's word so that the God who will not violate His own word will judge us and punish us according to it. Satan simply got Eve to disobey God. Everything else that befell them, their punishment and judgment was from God.

Redefining marriage so that it embraces or represents what its designer and creator clearly did not intend is not fixing or improving it. It is destroying it. Jesus said to His disciples in Matt. 5:13,

Ye are the salt of the earth when the salt has lost its savor (or saltiness or ability to perform or fulfill its purpose) *it is good for nothing, except to be cast out and trampled under the foot of men.*

When Satan gets finished with marriage, he will wreck and destroy as many as he can, in as many ways as he can. Then with his redefining and changing of roles he will make many worthless. The one thing we can be sure of is this, it will not in anyway represent Jesus Christ and His church, which is God's intended purpose. Neither will it serve in that state to remind God of His promise, another of its purposes.

It will become totally meaningless. Like Eve, we are being setup by Satan to be rejected by God and cast out. Society may find other uses for marriage; they may use it to determine tax breaks or other benefit eligibility. But to the God who established it and its true value it will be worthless, like salt without savor something to be destroyed along with everything else. "Professing themselves to be wise they have become fools." *Rom. 1:22.*

CHAPTER 16

What should your response be?

Now consider this. You have an enemy that despises and hates you beyond words. He hates you so much he would kill his own family to hurt you. Almost every evil or disaster that has ever befallen you was caused by him. Suddenly this person comes to you and wants to buy your house. Would you sell it to him? This person has not changed and seeks to destroy you with their every breath. Would you sell? What if he is offering you double the price? Now because you were not planning to sell he will have to convince you with many different approaches. He may say things like the house is no good, or the neighborhood is going down, or the man across the street hates you, taxes are too high, crime, drugs, poor schools, the mayor is a bum or you can take my money and get a better one. Would you sell it to him?

The wise person would say no. Even if they are not immediately able to figure out their enemy's real motive, they know he does not seek their wellbeing. They know it is not in their best interest and would most likely hurt them later. (Maybe unknown to them; oil was discovered in the area and their property will be worth 100 times its value in weeks).

To couples I say, the first thing to understand is that your spouse is not your enemy. Your common enemy is Satan.

Eph.6:12. *For we wrestle not against flesh and blood, but against principalities, against powers, against the rulers of the darkness of this world, against spiritual wickedness in high places.*

He who has sought your destruction from birth is not now seeking your wellbeing. If he wants you out of your marriage; if he wants it to fail, knowing him should be all the motivation you need to make your marriage work.

Though he will point out and have you focus on your mate's faults, he may cause you to fixate on some guy or girl on the job, down the block, or in some group you belong to. He does not seek your happiness. Like Eve we flirt with our own destruction.

By getting married you dare to become the symbol that he hates most on this earth. He now hates you even more for this. Like he did to Eve he will attempt to do to you. He will lie, con and trick you into your own destruction and the destruction of your marriage.

Satan made one major miscalculation in the Garden of Eden and at Calvary. He totally underestimated the power of love. (Always keep in mind that Jesus does not mirror Adam but rather Adam was made to mirror Jesus). Satan knew that Adam knew the truth and understood the real consequences of his actions. Satan figured that there is no way Adam would give up paradise to go after Eve; no way would he choose to die for this woman. There would be no offspring, no race of man. God failed. Satan won.

Satan was wrong.

Again at Calvary, rather before Calvary we see Satan speaking through Peter telling Jesus that suffering was not for Him. *Matt. 16:23*. Jesus recognizing Satan responded: *"Get thee behind me Satan. Thou are an offence to me."* Peter said it, but Jesus knew that it was Satan speaking through him. Satan was not finished there however; for while Jesus was hanging on the cross we hear Satan repeatedly saying, if thou are the Christ come down off that cross and save yourself. He said this through the thief and also through those taunting Him from the foot of the cross. The phrasing may be different but the sentiment is the same as Peter's. We therefore conclude, the source must be the same.

Now if Satan was the one speaking through Peter and the people who were trying to get Jesus to abandon His purpose or mission, what in the world was he up to? Let us take a closer look and see why it was so important for Jesus to fail. Make no mistake, Satan wanted to kill Jesus, but if death is the result of sin, how do you kill a sinless person?

Take a look at these three scriptures and see if they help to shed some light.

First, look at 1 Cor. 13:1-3...*and though I give my body to be burned, and have not love, it profiteth me nothing.*
Next, take a look at 1 John 3:15. *whosoever hateth his brother is a murderer.*
Lastly, we look at Job 1:9-11....*[11]But put forth thine hand now, and touch all that he hath, and he will curse thee to thy face.*

Beginning with the last, we see Job the only person beside Jesus, Enoch and Noah in the bible called perfect being set up for testing. Remember we said Satan is a corrupter. Note that here with Job Satan's real challenge was to get Job to curse God to His face. Though he tortured Job to the brink of death he was not out to kill him. He was out to corrupt him. He was trying to get him to sin. Again remember, everything that's in the bible is there because in some way it points to Christ.

Satan knew that the wages of sin is death. He also knew that all his attempts to get Christ to sin had failed. I believe Satan is wise enough to realize that attempting to kill a sinless man could prove quite futile. Death is the wages of sin, not the result of injuries. When you put all these variables together Satan's only real chance of success was to get Jesus to sin that death may take Him out.

First, through Peter he tried to get Jesus to disobey His Father and not chose to die. When that failed, Satan set out to make absolutely sure that the unspeakable horror of Jesus' torture and crucifixion would not. After His abandonment by His friends, Jesus was lied on: He was spat on, slapped in the face and punched. Next, a crown of thorns was pressed on His head, sending its spikes down to his skull. They accentuated this with a purple robe so they could ridicule, mock and make fun of him as some pathetic wanna-be king. This was only their warm up.

Jesus was then scourged. This term describes the shredding of his body beyond recognition with whips woven with bits of glass, bones, and metals. After his scourging, He was paraded through the streets carrying a massive cross. Insults were added to injuries by having Him displayed with two known thieves at the place of His death.

Upon arrival at the designated location they pounded nails through his hands and feet fastening him to the cross. The foot of the cross was then planted in the earth, hoisting Him in the air for more ridicule and taunting. For six mind-numbing hours He was made to hang by nails on this cross, as the crowd teases and dared Him to come down, if He was who He claimed to be. While the weight of his body caused the nails to tear His flesh, He hung there. He hung there for hours in indescribable anguish, with as far as Satan was concerned, nothing to think about but all that He had done for these people and how they chose to repay Him. He had to hate at least one.

Military official, torture experts, and psychologists alike agree that extreme torture will cause its victims to say, do or confess to anything, even a lie to alleviate their suffering. For sure Satan had Jesus where he wanted Him.

Satan never thought Jesus could love us enough to suffer for us the way He did. He never thought Jesus would love us enough to die and go to hell, the only way to free us from the power of death, hell and the grave. But just to make sure, first he used Jesus' own close friend and trusted companion to betray Him. Satan was using the very people that Jesus was dying for to kill Him, taunt, tease and jeer Him. Satan figured there was no way anyone could love people like this. He figured this is the point where Jesus would say, "They just aren't worth it."

Satan figured this would be his finest moment, the place where hatred triumphed, the place where love failed. Looking back to the first two of those three earlier scriptures, this is all Satan needed. If he had gotten Jesus to hate even just one of His tormentors and murderers, according to 1 John 3:15 the bible says, He would be a murderer. Then also according to 1 Corinthians 13, His sacrifice would have profited nothing. Jesus would have failed; we would be forever lost. Satan would have won.

With no stone left unturned, Satan waited by the cross to celebrate his certain victory, when Jesus' anger, resentment, hurt, and hatred would erupt.

Instead however he heard, "Father forgive them for they know not what they do." **At the place where Satan expected love to fail, love erupted and came shining through like a thousand noonday suns on a cloudless day.**

Satan was wrong.

Still, Satan is not finished. To every couple I say, Satan has made certain calculations and assumptions regarding your marriage, and about the strength of your love. Satan has calculated and assumed that if your spouse acts up in a certain way, fail to do certain things you expect, treat or fail to treat you a certain way, your love will fail. He has attacked your finances, because he believes your ambition will cause your love to evaporate and fail, during your time of economic hardship or poverty. He has attacked your health, because he believes you are too selfish to love, care and cherish your spouse through sickness.

He has attacked your ego and self esteem: The wife is made to feel unattractive and undesirable: The husband is made to feel less than a man, sometimes by his own spouse. Satan figured your pride would not stand for it and your love would fail. He has used your foes, friends and family to attack your marriage attempting to reduce your spouse in your eyes. He figured with your close external bonds, tight friendships, and need for others approval, this would be too much for your love to overcome and it would fail.

He has made many other assumptions regarding your marriage and the strength of your love. He calculated the impact of certain attitudes and behavior by your children, certain responsibilities or career choices. These are just some of the things he will use to accomplish his desire, which is the failure of your love, and the destruction of you and your marriage. He desires to break the unbreakable, to separate the inseparable. Mark 10:9 *what therefore God has joined together, let not man put asunder.*

Like mine, I believe Satan will hit yours and every marriage. There have been or will be times when you think that you have taken his best shot, only to find out that he was just warming up. This is my prayer for you. I pray that after Satan have launched every rocket, missile, and bomb in his arsenal at you, your love will not fail. After all the dust and smoke have settled from his attacks on your marriage, you will still be standing. I pray that you will be standing with your spouse held tighter and closer than ever before. I pray that you and your spouse will be able to look Satan in the face and say, "I know what you calculated. I know what you assumed and what you thought but... Satan you were wrong!" You will turn to 1 Cor.13:4-8 and say it loud to his face, "**True love never fails.**"

Just as Adam, with everything to lose, held onto his wife for love's sake, and Job after losing everything, held onto his faith and integrity for love sake. Just as Jesus having nothing to lose, endured everything that Satan could throw at and on Him, went to hell and back for love's sake, and for our sake. May we also having done all to stand, stand for love sake, and for Jesus sake, thereby being for the entire world to see, a true reflection of Jesus Christ, whose image we are called to bear.

CHAPTER 17

The Bride of Christ

What should the church's response be? In light of what we have discussed so far, in light of what God has revealed there are two ways to respond to the above question. The first is: Being the bride of Christ, what should the church look like or embody in its relationship and behavior towards the ultimate groom, Jesus Christ, the only true Mr. Perfect to ever live? The second way to respond, which we will look at in the next chapter is: What should the church be doing for couples and for marriages in light of the present distress, in light of Satan's all out assault on this sacred God ordained institution?

We begin with the first because it is easier. What should the church's behavior towards Christ be? Important to note at this juncture is the fact that becoming a part of the bride of Christ means to enter into a personal relationship with Christ. Now I have observed that many churches are making some of the same mistakes that couples make in their marriages, mistakes that can lead to divorce.

At this point I guess I could start listing all these things that I perceive to be wrong with the churches. However, I will not. A federal agent once said the way they identified counterfeit is not by trying to study counterfeits, but rather by studying the genuine item. The best way I can think of accomplishing a study of the real thing is with a quick skim through the bible. I will note from several places what God word has commanded a wife to be towards her husband. I will then see how the church can and should embody this towards Christ.

The Church: God's helper Gen.2: 18-20

Woman was created to be a help meet for man. Here the word tells us that woman was created to be a helper suited for or compatible to man. Also we see in 1 Corinthians 11:9. *Neither was the man created for the woman but the woman for the man.* When a man chooses a wife he is hoping for someone that will first share, then help him to realize his life mission, purpose or vision. The sharing of the vision is important because then it becomes their vision instead of his.

The bible says of the church: We are the body of Christ. *1 Corinthians 12.* In John 15, Jesus refers to Himself as the vine and us as the branches. This chapter goes on to show the love relationship between Christ and His church, and also that we are called to continue what He has started. It further shows that He will always be with us. We will be working as a team but because it is His mission that has now become ours, we are therefore His helper.

The church therefore is called to be a helper compatible to Christ. We are called to be Jesus to the world. One person puts it this way: The only Jesus they will ever see is the one they see in you and me. This is how it works. Throughout scripture, whenever Jesus called a believer, they had to abandon their old life and embrace His cause to be a true disciple. In Jesus' words, *"take up your cross and follow Me."* Mat.16:24. The church is called as the bride of Christ to embody through our commitment, dedication, love and devotion to Jesus and His cause, what the wife should be to her husband. *See also 1Corinthians 7:34.*

Jesus calls Himself the Good Shepherd, and before His departure His instruction to Peter who was to lead the others was to feed His sheep. Our mission as the church is first to know and possess the heart of Christ through our personal relationship with Him. *Phil. 2:5*. Next, we should diligently and prayerfully seek out His will and purpose for our lives. Just as Jesus praying to His Father said, "Yet not My will but Thy will be done". *Luke 22:42*. So also we are instructed to pray. *Luke 11:2*. Once we've discovered God's will, we then seek with all our heart, mind and strength to fulfill it. Then like Jesus the church will be able to say, "I must be about my Father's / (husband's) business." *Luk.2:49*.

Submitted to and subjected to Jesus (Eph. 5:22: 1Peter 3:15)

Possibly the greatest example of what these scriptures mean by wives being submitted to and subjected to your husband is the life of the apostle Paul. He outlines this in Philippians 3:4-9. He said all that he was raised and trained to be, which he dearly loved and esteemed, he abandoned and counted as dung to embrace and fulfill the cause of Jesus Christ. His statement, "What will thou have me to do Lord", when Jesus met Paul on the road to Damascus is what submission sounds like.

Unlike the gospel being preached today in many of our churches depicting Jesus as the servant waiting in the church with an apron to say to us: What will you have me to do? (This is a can of worms I had better not touch). Suffice it to say, this is not so, but rather it is us who surrender to His lordship. We are the ones who ought to be saying to Christ, "what will You have me to do Lord." God's blessings are tied to our obedience to His word, not our ability to believe for our greed, or simply patiently wait in line for our turn. *Deuteronomy 28:1*.

A church submitted to Jesus reflects His heartbeat, continuing what He started. It is a ministry committed to a cause and not an image of itself. It is one committed to establishing the name of Jesus Christ and the message of salvation, not making a name for itself and having the grandest facility. The submitted church is one driven by love and compassion and not pride and ambition. Submitted is Jesus praying to His Father in the Garden of Gethsemane *"..yet not my will but thy will be done"*.

Submission and subjection to Jesus must be the posture and reality in the church, not just as a model for the world only. It also serves to protect us from the pride that caused the downfall of Satan and so many others. Couple this with the words of James 4:6, Proverbs 15:25, Malachi 4:1 and many other such scriptures, submission to Jesus is an absolute essential in the life of every believer. If we fail to submit, then Jesus is really not Lord of our lives. Throughout scripture as in John 14:34-35 & 15:10, Jesus made it clear that we are truly His only if we keep His commandments.

The Virtuous Wife (Proverbs 30:10-31)

Solomon here describes the perfect wife. This image also should be perfectly reflected by the church. Truth is, the early church started by the apostles was a picture of this woman. This was a church where they had all things in common. A system was put in place where those who had, voluntarily brought it in to the leaders to be distributed, that there remained no unmet need among them.

Even as Jesus became the fulfillment of the needs of the people, so too should His bride the church. Jesus fed their hungry, healed the sick, became their light in darkness and the way to those that are lost. (By the way, that was the state of all of us). Proverbs 30:27 said of the virtuous woman that she attended well to the needs of her family. Every church should pay careful attention to the words of this proverb and seek in every way and by all means to reflect this image. The bride of Christ should be a nurturing, caring, loving and compassionate oasis for all in need of refuge, relief or refreshing. All the things that are the heartbeat of God should flourish in her. God's children should find their every need met in her because of her resourcefulness, industriousness and wisdom.

Every church leadership should study carefully the character of this virtuous woman as described by Solomon in Proverbs. Paul in 1 Corinthians 3:10-13 explains that the foundation is already laid, but it will take wisdom on each builder's part to build what God is looking for. Wisdom is needed on the part of leadership to ensure that an infrastructure is put in place. This infrastructure should ultimately produce for Christ a ministry with all the characteristic of the virtuous woman.

When I speak of a ministry I am speaking of the church not just an outreach. An outreach can target a specific need and that's all they are called to do. Many times these targeted outreaches are the limbs of churches. Many times in small and new churches because of economic constraints they lack the resources to meet all the needs and do all the things needed. They should never however lack the will and desire to do all that's needed, so that they may reflect the image of Christ.

We are a team, Jesus said in St. John 15:5. Therefore, I believe where there is the will and desire Christ will make the way. He'll open doors for us to build the church or ministry that will cause the groom, Jesus Christ, to take joy, delight and pleasure in his bride.

Like the bride who stayed faithful to her husband in the hard times, he will have no problem trusting her when he has made it big, so it is with Christ. Ministries that remain faithful to the cause and call of Jesus during the tough times, when it is most tempting to compromise and deviate for the sake of ease or greed, Jesus said He will entrust them with much. *Rev. 3:8.*

The church, the perfected bride of Christ, should undoubtedly model for the world the biblical image of the perfect wife. It should also always possess within it the church's only true identifier: love for each other even as the groom loves us.

CHAPTER 18

How Should The Church Respond To Satan's Attack On Marriage?

It would be both arrogant and naïve of me to believe or imply that I have all the answers to this question. What I offer here are some observations and a few suggestions on where to get more help. The first point I must make is that doing nothing, or pretending that there is not a crisis in our culture in regards to marriage is not an option. This I feel would amount to nothing less than assisting Satan in his mission. Also the fallout from this battle will impact every area of society. Since Marriage and family are the nucleus and building blocks of our society, we will ultimately bring our entire civilization to the ground if it is destroyed. Therefore, whether you know it or not, we are all involved and are a part of this war on marriage.

The good news is, there are a number of churches and ministries out there that are doing a remarkable job in the struggle to save marriages. The bad news is, far too many are still clueless or complacent. Some churches are even contributing to the demise of marriage in our society, by their policies and practices. This is truly tragic.

We have already demonstrated God's stand regarding marriage and His support of it from scripture. Knowing this, the church, God's representative here should also in its practices and policies demonstrate a clear and unwavering stand in support of this institution. The church should demonstrate this support for marriage and family in its investments and agendas. Our reality is this, if there is no counter balance to Satan's relentless attack on marriage the battle is lost.

As our government passes more laws to weaken marriage, and our society promotes more politically correct social agendas detrimental to marriage, the church must counter. The church needs to counter lies with truth. We need to promote marriage for what it really is. We need to promote Gods design for marriage. There is much the church can do such as:

- Stop sanctioning divorces outside of God's allowances.
- Properly counsel those entering marriage, arming them with truth.
- Not remarry those separated outside of God's allowable.
- Develop intervention programs.
- Create support systems and mentoring programs for couples.
- Celebrate and empower couples with enrichment programs.
- Provide parenting support, training, and assistance.
- Provide financial counseling, and economic assistance when able.

In an increasingly godless society, one desperately trying to remove God from the equation, marriage as He designed it must go. There is just too much to do with Him wrapped up in it. Marriage was meant to be a lifetime covenant between a man and a woman, to love, cherish and serve each other until death. Marriage is a mystical, physical and spiritual union that is tied to our Creator in many more ways than the obvious. In the Garden of Eden God took one (Adam) and from him made two. In the marriage ceremony God reverses Eden in a mystical way not observable to the eyes: Here He takes two and makes them one. Read carefully how Jesus puts it in Mark 10:6-9.

> *But at the beginning of creation God 'made them male and female. *[7]*'For this reason a man will leave his father and mother and be united to his wife,*[1] [8]*and the two will become one flesh. So they are no longer two, but one. *[9]*Therefore what God has joined together, let man not separate.*

After you have stood before a minister and witnesses, after you have taken that solemn oath or vow and prayed, note carefully that God does the joining. Therefore whether or not your society or your government gives you a license you are married before God. Whether they give you benefits or not you are married before God. This also means that if they do give it and then take it back as in the case of divorce, because they did not join you, you are still married before God. This also is made plain by Jesus in Mark 10:11-12...

> *Anyone who divorces his wife and marries another woman commits adultery against her.*
> [12]*And if she divorces her husband and marries another man, she commits adultery.*

Paul also in 1Cor. 7 gives his allowable grounds for divorce and remarriage. Other preachers have created their own list claiming I suppose to be following Paul's example. I am sure also that with the present state of moral decay, and the ever increasing wickedness in our society, that a few more grounds could be added. The problem I have found is that regardless how conservative and restrictive a list we create, every couple wanting out of their marriage will find their justification in that list.

Once we begin to justify divorce and remarriage outside the boundaries in the bible, who will establish the new boundary and where will those new boundaries be? The church should be about seeking all possible means to strengthen and preserve marriages, not help couples find all possible escape routes.

CHAPTER 19

Becoming an 'Antidevil'

I believe this is the place where I should tell you how Cathy and I are doing now after fifteen years. In light of all that God has revealed to me. My guess is you're probably expecting me to say that we are now the perfect couple, with the perfect marriage, and no struggles whatsoever. This however is neither fairytale nor fiction so I can't. The fact is Cathy and I believe we have a great thing going. We sometimes still find ourselves on the roller coaster. The difference now is we're learning how to enjoy the ride. We've learned to hang onto each other when it gets scary, and celebrate like crazy when it's going great. Getting off is no longer even a consideration. We now understand who our common enemy is and know what it takes to win.

One key to victory in any battle is, understanding your opponent's strengths and weaknesses or knowing your enemy. Having examined Satan's track record and what the bible says about him, we have a good idea what we are up against. We've seen Satan attack many people. We have seen him hit them with everything he has. We then saw those who remained true to God, and did not do what Satan was hoping, triumph and became victors. Some examples of these champions are Job, Joseph, Daniel, and Jesus, to name a few.

Being tempted, tested, and tried is something that happens to all of us. The bible actually says, *"Think it not strange concerning the fiery trial that will try you."* Peter 4:12. Satan is desperately trying to get you to act up or react contrary to God's word, so that you might be judged and punished even as he was. He is hoping the circumstances of your life will drive or push you to reject God and His word. He is greatly desirous of your company in hell.

The understanding that lies and deception are Satan's weapons of choice means that the battleground is the mind. This means that in the middle of your situation, whatever it is: problems, pain or pleasure, he will find a way to speak into your life. He will be trying to convince you that now is not the time to think about God and what He wants. He'll be trying to convince you that it is all about you, your pleasure, your happiness, your relief, your possessions, your goals and dreams or your revenge.

He'll be trying to convince you that God cannot be good if He allows this or that situation to occur. Also, if He were really good then He would want you to do whatever, just because it feels good. Better yet, how can you deny yourself when you can't even be sure that there is a God? These and many other lies and doubts will Satan bombard you with, just as he did with Eve when he asked her: "Did God really say that?"

Satan will always have someone within striking distance of you to reinforce the negatives, speaking lies into your heart and mind. We see that for Eve there was the serpent, for Job, his three best friends, and for Jesus, there were too many to mention, including his disciples at times.

You may have heard of the antichrist. Allow me to introduce you to the antidevil. Satan needs and is always able to find someone close to you to get at you. Someone to tap into your weaknesses and press you until you break. (David wrote about his unbearable experience in Psalm 55:12-13).

Similarly, God also has someone within striking distance of you. Jesus, before His ascension, told His disciples He would not leave them comfortless but would send them a Helper. The terminology used in the scripture speaks of one that comes along side to help. Even as Satan uses people to get to you, God also uses people to get to you. The person that God chooses to use in your life, to counter the power of Satan bent on your failure and destruction, I refer to as your 'antidevil'.

Wives and husbands are meant to be the antidevil in each other's lives. Note that just like the Holy Spirit was given to us as a helper, Eve was given to Adam as a helper suited for him. Someone sent alongside to help. We also see in Ecc. 4:9-12 where it states that two is better than one because they are there to help each other up if either falls. Couples were meant to be each other's helper and since they are joined together by God they were meant to be God's instrument of help in each other's lives.

A husband or a wife can be the strength of their spouse or they can be their spouse's strongest weakness. This is solely contingent upon who we allow to use us: God or the devil. 'How do I determine who uses me?' you ask. That is a very good question with a simple answer. The one whose tools you possess will be the one that uses you. God or the devil will work with what is inside the toolbox of the heart. *Keep your heart with diligence for out of it proceeds the issues of life.* Prov.4:23.

To be the antidevil in someone's life you must possess the tools the Holy Spirit needs. This tool is like a Swiss knife: a single instrument with many parts to it. The bible calls it fruit. The fruit is love, but it is more like a fruit basket as described in Gal. 5:22-23 and 1Cor. 13. This ingredient, fruit, or tool just happens to be the number one ingredient in marriage: love.

The same way the devil uses people to speak lies into our lives that ultimately produce death, the Holy Spirit will use someone to speak God's truth into our lives that will lead to life. The bible says we are to speak the truth in love to each other. When Satan's lies have left us wounded, and crushed, without hope and ready to die, the Holy Spirit will use someone to speak life, hope, and healing into our lives. That someone is your 'antidevil'.

For the married couple, by virtue of their common love, the spouse should be God's first choice for the position of antidevil in the other's life. It is important first that we recognize the great need for this ministry in each other's life. Next, we must have a desire to help, then strive to be that instrument of hope and grace first in the life of our spouse and then in the lives of others.

When couples commit to being the antidevil in each other's lives something magical happens. They fill such a great need in each other, that they are more interdependent and they become even closer. We become for each other the person that speaks life into death, hope into despair, peace into chaos, strength into weakness, comfort and healing into pain and love and encouragement into fear and distrust. We so desperately need such a person in our lives that should we find someone like this we want to hold onto them for life. This is the person who not only sees the best in us but also brings out the best in us.

When we allow God to use us as the antidevil in our spouse's life we also benefit. We find ourselves with the best spouse around. This position requires diligence. The devil will not miss an opportunity to speak death, doom, fear and despair into our lives. We therefore should not let opportunities pass to speak love, hope, and comfort into each other's lives.

We should also remember to speak in a language that will be clearly understood by the person. A person under stress or feeling undervalued does not want to guess or wonder. Many times our actions will speak louder than our words. Meaning, a person stressed out because of work will more clearly understand you care and love them if you roll up your sleeves and help them. When 'I love you' is not clear enough, try something tangible like flowers or a gift.

The fact that Satan will never quit or retire from trying to destroy us should not scare us. It should only serve to remind us that as an antidevil neither can we. There will be times when we might see our loved ones going down and want to say *not again* or *I am tired of this*. The devil never gets tired of trying to trip us, bring us down or destroy us. We cannot weary God. Our heavenly Father never gets tired of picking us up when we fall. Therefore neither will we stop being God's antidevil in each other's life.

To love someone that loves you proves nothing. True love can only be measured by the size of the sacrifice demanded and the amount of forgiveness required.

The bible declares in Malachi 2:14-17 that God hates divorce. The truth that we must live out, the truth that we must clearly communicate to our adversary the devil is this. As long as there is true love, the God-established institution of marriage on this earth will never cease, because TRUE LOVE NEVER FAILS.

CHAPTER 20

The Grand finale

To every married couple and those aspiring to be married, allow me to commend you on being or desiring to be God's symbol on the earth. You may not have thought about it that way before, but it is what you will become. Now that we've begun to grasp the reality that so much of what we hold dear as a society is as a result of, or is sustained by marriage and family, there is more. It is important that we understand something about the destruction of Sodom and Gomorrah. The angels of God came to destroy them because of their sinful and evil practices. Homosexuality just happened to be one of the sinful practices or indulgence of a people blessed with plenty, and lots of free time. *Ezek. 16:49.*

Their prosperity made pleasure seeking their only pastime. Regardless how debasing or degrading the practice, if they thought it might be pleasurable they would indulge. They were pretty much the way we are today. They would not entertain any argument or discussion that they believe might curtail or restrict their freedom to do as they please. They totally disregarded Lot. They probably thought of him as out of touch or intolerant, because he did not approve of their sinful lifestyle. However, this was not the reason Sodom was ultimately destroyed. God's final reason for destroying the city is found in Gen. 18:22-32. Here God told Abraham that He knew the people were wicked, but for ten righteous people the entire city would be spared.

Despite the original intent, those cities would have been spared for ten righteous. Sodom and Gomorrah in the final analysis were therefore ultimately destroyed because ten righteous people could not be found there. Do not let this be the fate of your city, town, or nation. Stand. Having done all to stand, stand.

Still, the greatest tragedy would be, for you to faithfully represent and embody the symbol and then not be a part of its true actualization. By this I mean that when Jesus Christ, the ultimate Groom comes for His bride you are not a part of that celebration, and as a result never get to fully realize or see what the fight was all about, though you defended it well. People will be thrown from the wedding feast because they were not wearing their wedding garment. *Matt. 22:11-14.* If you have not done so as yet, please get to know Jesus Christ as your Lord and Savior. There is just too much at stake.

What's Really at Stake

Some may read this book and say maybe the broom is just a broom. Maybe the similarities and references drawn are just coincidences. My best response to this would be as one of my former pastors would say, "And maybe the Lexus is the result of a random explosion in a junk yard"

How can you trust the bible, a book written by a man, many say? I will respond to this by sharing a truth that according to a Rutgers University professor I met is almost a statistical impossibility.

The truth be told, the bible from cover to cover represents the greatest love story ever compiled or written. The bible is comprised of sixty six different books that tell one story. It was written under the inspiration of the Holy Spirit by over forty different authors from all walks of life: shepherds, farmers, tent-makers, fishermen, physicians, priests, philosophers and kings. It was written over a period of some 1,500 years, from around 1450 B.C. (before Christ) to about 100 A.D. (In the year of our Lord or after the birth of Christ). Also the bible was written in three different languages: Hebrew, Aramaic, and Greek. This signifies the influence of different cultures and places. Despite these differences in occupation and language, despite the span of years it took to write it, the bible is an extremely cohesive and unified book that tells one amazing story.

It is the story of the indescribable, incomprehensible, unparalleled, mind-blowing love of the Wonder of wonders, the omnipotent God of the universe for His unworthy creation. The story tells of the mighty God whose favorite creation and object of His love, (man) betrays Him. Man in rebellion then sides with God's enemy, who desires to overthrow the King of Kings and Lord of the universe.

It is the story of love so strong that not even death, at the hands of the object of His love could destroy or diminish it. It tells that when God dressed Himself in flesh and came in the person of Jesus Christ to tell them of His love, He was brutally murdered by the ones He loved, yet it did not diminish His passionate love for them.

The love story continues, telling of Him coming back from the dead only to pour out more love on His double-crossing, backstabbing creation, though the majority continued to reject him. This love story then tells us not of Him destroying them all, but of him reuniting with all those who accept His proposal, receive His love and in return fall in love with Him, which is evidenced by their obedience to Him.

This final uniting of God and His creation through Jesus Christ is referred to as a marriage. This uniting is what is meant to be represented in the earth by the marriage of a man and a woman. Every bride wants the wedding to remember and every groom wants the honeymoon to remember. Well in this story it tells of a honeymoon that lasts not one or two weeks not even a month but seven years.

What about the venue? The story tells of a place called heaven: the splendor, beauty and indescribable grandeur none can even come close to describing. It says:

"Eye hath not seen, nor ear heard, neither have entered into the heart of man, the things which God hath prepared for them that love him". 1 Cor. 2:9.

There is no physical description of any kind in the bible or anywhere of heaven. Growing up in church over the years I've heard it described as having walls of jasper and streets of gold. The truth is they are only describing a mere trinket that will be brought back from heaven by the bride and Groom. They are describing the New Jerusalem not heaven.

Heaven is also described as a place of unspeakable joy. Sex is God's gift to couples after marriage. It is that which so many are selling their souls for. But the most earth-shaking, senses-exploding sex in the world is a cold shower in winter in comparison to the glory, joy and ecstasy to be realized, revealed and enjoyed by the believers in heaven. People will walk away from their marriages because of mere inconvenience. But the bible says that a lifetime of pure hellish torture will be considered light afflictions and nothing, an incredibly small price to pay for the glory that shall be revealed in us, when the bride gets to heaven. The story ends with the Groom and bride returning to earth destroying all His enemies, subduing the earth and reigning over it together, living happily ever after.

This love story is what husbands and wives joined together by God are meant to represent and model to the world. While the world looks for love in all the wrong places, God invites us all to be a part of the greatest love story ever, to experience truly the greatest love of all. We have been called to love, live, and declare this truth.

We were created in the image of the awesome God to show forth His praise and glory. It is a glory so incredible we can't even fathom much less display or explain. Therefore, the best we can do is offer Him ourselves and ask Him to demonstrate or show Himself through us.

We are called to become living epistles that will be read by all. This means that when they look at us, they must read and understand from our love for each other and for our Lord: "For God so love the world" or this is how God loves you. The world is no longer listening but it is forever watching. It is time to give them something to look at. It's time to show them what true love looks like, God's love.

Beginning with married couples, the standard bearers, designated keepers of the sacred flame, earth's symbolic reminders of God's unbreakable promise, let everyone who has accepted Jesus' proposal, embracing Him as Lord and Savior go forth and sincerely represent Him. Go love someone just like God loves you.

APPENDIX

Hopefully after having read this book you are now being convicted by God to take a stand. You are now fired up by your understanding of what is at stake. Now that you have a compelling reason to fight, you are ready to do battle to strengthen and defend the God ordained institution of marriage.

Only you are not sure where to begin, what to hit first, what to do, and how to do it. Though there are some "how to do" and what to do" suggestions in this book, it was meant to be primarily a "what for" and "why to" book. Now however, to fight you want to arm yourself with the knowledge, proven skill sets and approaches that will ensure victory in your particular area of struggle: Whether it is your own family or marriages in general. The bible says, *my people are destroyed because of a lack of knowledge. Hosea 4:6.* We fight to win.

A search on Amazon.com for books on marriage will yield over 7000 results. This is enough to overwhelm anyone. I am not going to point you to one particular book because I do not know the particular battle you are fighting. Instead I am going to point you to ministries that for over twenty years their almost sole purpose for existing is to fight for, support, defend and strengthen marriages and families.

They are worldwide and able to provide you with books, tapes, CDs, DVDs, brochures, counselors and more, to address or assist you in any area of interest or struggle relating to marriage and family. There are other wonderful ministries around that can also provide support and various forms of assistance. However, I highly recommend these two because I have used their resources and my own marriage and ministry have benefited from their programs.

    The first is FamilyLife Ministries
            P O Box 7111
            Little Rock, Arkansas, 72223
            Tel. (800) 358-6329 or
            Online at www.Familylife.com.

    The other is Focus on the Family
            Colorado Springs, Co, 80995
            Tel. (800) A-family or 232-6459 also
            Online at www.Family.org

ABOUT THE AUTHOR

Ainsley is the youngest of four children. He has two brothers and one sister. His father died when he was four years old. Ainsley credits all that he is to his Heavenly Father's faithfulness, love and His answers to the prayers of his praying mother, Viris Reynolds who also went to be with her Lord on April 11, 2007.

Ainsley is an ordained Elder. He is married to wife Catherine for over 15 years, and they are the proud parents of daughter Kassandra and son Eric. Ainsley has been working in ministry for over 22 years. He has held many different positions in ministry from Sunday school teacher to his most recent role as Pastor. In 15 years of marriage Ainsley and Cathy have gone from fairy tale, to melt down, to mountain top and back. As a minister and then as a pastor, Ainsley has been counseling married and pre-married couples for over 10 years.

The driving forces in Ainsley's life are, first, his passionate love for Jesus Christ, which is the fuel behind all that he does in ministry. Second to this is his love for his family, which is his motivation to be a good husband and father. Thirdly, is his desire to see people come to know Jesus as He really is, and have their lives transformed by this knowledge.

Ainsley has taken his many years of experience as a marriage counselor and his fifteen years of hands-on experience as a husband and father. He then mixed in twenty plus years of studying God's word, overlaid it with prayer to produce what promises to be a great weapon in the battle to save marriages.

Made in the USA